INSTAGRAM MARKETING SECRETS

How to go viral, growing followers, become an influencer and make money

Dave Miller

© **Copyright 2019 by Dave Miller- All rights reserved.**

This document is geared towards providing exact and reliable information in regards to the topic and issue covered. The publication is sold with the idea that the publisher is not required to render accounting, officially permitted, or otherwise, qualified services. If advice is necessary, legal or professional, a practiced individual in the profession should be ordered.

- From a Declaration of Principles which was accepted and approved equally by a Committee of the American Bar Association and a Committee of Publishers and Associations. In no way is it legal to reproduce, duplicate, or transmit any part of this document in either electronic means or in printed format. Recording of this publication is strictly prohibited and any storage of this document is not allowed unless with written permission from the publisher. All rights reserved.

The information provided herein is stated to be truthful and consistent, in that any liability, in terms of inattention or otherwise, by any usage or abuse of any policies, processes, or directions contained within is the solitary and utter responsibility of the recipient reader. Under no circumstances will any legal responsibility or blame be held against the publisher for any reparation, damages, or monetary loss due to the information herein, either directly or indirectly.

Respective authors own all copyrights not held by the publisher.

The information herein is offered for informational purposes solely, and is universal as so the presentation of the information is without contract or any type of guarantee assurance.

The trademarks that are used are without any consent, and the publication of the trademark is without permission or backing by the trademark owner. All trademarks and brands within this book are for clarifying purposes only and are the owned by the owners themselves, not affiliated with this document.

CONTENTS

CHAPTER 1: BEGINNERS 6

    1.1 INTRODUCTION 6

    1.2 WHY INSTAGRAM MARKETING IS KEY TO ECOMMERCE SUCCESS? 9

    1.3 THE INSTAGRAM ALGORITHM 10

    1.4 IDENTIFYING YOUR GOALS AND OBJECTIVES 13

    1.5 HOW TO CREATE AN INSTAGRAM BUSINESS ACCOUNT? 14

    1.6 BUILD A CONSISTENT INSTAGRAM AESTHETIC 17

    1.7 WHY DO YOU USE INSTAGRAM TO MARKET? 19

    1.8 ROLE OF INSTAGRAM AS A MARKETING PLATFORM 23

CHAPTER 2: TEAM ORGANIZATION 30

    2.1 DEFINING YOUR IDEAL TEAM 31

    2.2 SUCCESSFULLY MERGING TASKS 35

CHAPTER 3: STEPPING IN 39

    3.1 BREAKING DOWN YOUR PLATFORM BARRIERS 39

    3.2 TARGETING THE AUDIENCE 41

    3.3 SERVING UP EXCLUSIVE CONTENT 45

    3.4 USING EDITING APPS 49

    3.5 STEPPING IN THE TRENDS 51

CHAPTER 4: MAKE MONEY FROM YOUR INTSAGRAM ACCOUNT ... 54

CHAPTER 5: MAINTAINING INSTAGRAM PROFILES 58

    5.1 VISUALIZE A STUNNING PROFILE 58

    5.2 POSTING HIGH-QUALITY CONTENT 58

    5.4 CREATE A SEAMLESS FEED 59

    5.5 CREATE A POSTING SCHEDULE 60

5.6 MAINTAIN YOUR STORY 61

5.7 SHOUT THEM OUT 67

5.8 POST BEHIND-THE-SCENE CONTENT 67

5.9 SHARE RESEARCH WARNING AND TRENDS 68

CHAPTER 6: GROWING FOLLOWERS 70

6.1 HOW TO GET MORE INSTAGRAM FOLLOWERS 70

6.2 ORGANIC FOLLOWERS A CRUCIAL PART 73

6.3 HASH TAGS AND THEIR EFFECTIVENESS 74

6.4 LINKING OUT TO CUSTOMIZED PAGES 78

6.5 HOW TO TRACK YOUR IMPRESSIONS, REACH, ENGAGEMENT, AND MORE 79

6.6 SOME OTHER TIPS FOR GROWING FOLLOWERS 81

CHAPTER 7: ADVERTISEMENT 86

7.1 LEARNING FOLLOWER PREFERENCES (USAGE OF ANALYTICS) 86

7.2 BUILD A FOLLOWING OF HIGHLY ENGAGED FANS 88

7.3 INSTAGRAM ADVERTISEMENT DOOR TO MARKETING 92

7.4 TARGETING OPTIONS FOR ADVERTISEMENT 99

7.5 FOCUSING ON CONTENT BEFORE INVESTING IN ADVERTISEMENT 100

7.6 DISCOUNTS AND PROMOTIONS 100

CHAPTER 8: VIDEO TELECASTS A SOURCE OF MARKETING 102

8.1 HOW TO USE INSTAGRAM LIVE FOR BUSINESS 102

8.2 USING IGTV FOR BUSINESS 105

8.3 TIPS FOR MAKING GREAT INSTAGRAM BUSINESS VIDEO POSTS 107

CHAPTER 9: BECOMING AN INFLUENCER 112

9.1 LEVERAGE SOCIAL MEDIA INFLUENCERS NATURALLY 112

9.2 HOW TO FIND THE RIGHT INFLUENCERS FOR YOUR BUSINESS? 113

9.3 WHY YOUR BUSINESS NEEDS AN INSTAGRAM INFLUENCER MARKETING STRATEGY? 115

9.5 EFFECTIVE STEPS FOR INFLUENCER MARKETING 118

9.6 CONNECTING WITH THE RIGHT INFLUENCERS 121

CHAPTER 10: HANDLING FAME (BEING VIRAL)..................123

10.1 USE A MONETIZATION TOOL 123

10.2 PARTNER UP WITH SUPPORTERS 123

10.3 RUNNING CONTESTS 124

10.4 FINDING A UNIQUE AND CREATIVE VOICE 128

10.5 INCREASING THE FAME 129

CHAPTER 11: REACTIONS AND REVIEWS 132

11.1 RUN YOUR INSTAGRAM AUDIT 132

CHAPTER 12: TIPS AND TRICKS 135

12.1 ASSIGN SOMEONE TO MONITOR MESSAGING CHANNELS 135

12.2 KEEP POST DRAFT ON HAND 135

12.3 DON'T BE AFRAID TO STIR THINGS UP 136

12.4 SOCIALIZE WELL WITH EXISTING FOLLOWERS 136

12.5 USE INSTAGRAM LIVE TO TEASE NEW PRODUCTS 137

12.6 LEAVING NOTHING BLANK 137

14. REFERENCES 143

CHAPTER 1: BEGINNERS

1.1 Introduction

Instagram advertising is how companies link with Instagram and market their offerings to their target audiences. Recently, brands have gained popularity as an innovative way to show off their cultures, recruit new staff, engage with consumers, and view goods in a new light.

Similar to Facebook and Twitter, there are a profile and newsfeed for everyone who creates an Instagram account. Through following, being followed, private messaging, and commenting on or enjoying photos or videos, users may communicate with each other. Instagram's in-app filters and editing features make the app unique because, to this point, it was the first product to provide in-app editing.

Instagram allows users to upload and edit photos and videos with different options for their profile. Instagram hosts hundreds of original filters that can be added to images by users. These preset filters make various modifications to the photos, including the addition of light, a warm or cold tone to the image, increasing or decreasing saturation, and more. Alternatively, in addition to using a third-party photo editor, users can edit images directly on the website. If you don't like a particular filter, you can use the editing feature of Instagram to change contrast, brightness, structure, warmth, saturation, sharpness, and more individually.

Instagram is a site for photo sharing and video sharing you can use to grow and develop your brand. Using Instagram, this course should act as an introduction to your company, from setting up an account to producing relevant content to using it as a powerful business resource. Back in 2010, it was like any other social platform when Instagram first appeared on the scene: full of selfies, pets, and food pictures. Fast forward to 2019, and Instagram's evolution from a simple photo-sharing platform to a full-on marketing channel is almost complete.

Now, look at some of the platform's latest features! Over the past year alone, Instagram has released dozens of new marketing tools, including advanced analytics, Instagram local notifications, and new ways to push Instagram Stories' traffic, and IGTV, the new standalone video platform. It helps create an Instagram profile, whether you're involved in e-commerce, education, or entertainment and publishing. But if you want to go forward, you need to learn how to manage your ratings and KPIs from the web (and the audience) inside and outside, such as what kind of content resonates, how to create a plan for Instagram Stories.

Instagram has vast opportunities for e-commerce companies seeking to highlight their goods. Whether through regular pictures, videos, or stories from Instagram, millions of businesses have discovered that creating a visible presence on Instagram will complement their e-commerce marketing.

Interestingly, followers of Instagram are more active than regular social media users. And while trends appear to indicate a decline in Instagram engagement, the site still delivers higher rates of business engagement compared to both Twitter and Facebook.

Yet users are more than just active on Instagram— they are also often online shoppers.

This shopping mentality makes Instagram users the perfect target because they are fully intentioned and quick to transform.

Another factor Instagram has to do with the site itself is so brilliant that Instagram has recently introduced a ton of new business-facing resources— and yeah, there's more to come! Whether through links to Instagram Stories or Instagram shopping updates, many of our online shopping encounters on Instagram will start (and end) as soon as possible.

It would be a mistake to think that Instagram is not your business because you are not selling e-commerce products! As well as its unique ability to move products, Instagram is also an incredible place for companies to build brand awareness and connect with new audiences (and potential customers).

Of course, if you want to create a marketing strategy that resonates with your target audience, first, you need to grasp how the Instagram algorithm works — Instagram, the new revolutionary photo-sharing app, makes posting the best pictures with the world more available than ever before. You will search, add digital filters, and post your photos on your Instagram feed and other social networking sites through social media software. For linking your Instagram profile, you can use Twitter, Snapchat, Pinterest, LinkedIn, Foursquare, and your email account. It makes it easy to post the images on multiple platforms all at once. As of September 2012, Instagram had 100 million registered users. To use Instagram, you need a Smartphone. You can click a picture and upload it to Instagram with your standard phone camera, or use the Instagram app (for iPhone) to take a picture. Add a filter, and you're ready to go!

After two years after the release of Instagram, Facebook made an offer of around $1 billion in cash and stock to purchase the active social media site in October 2010. The agreement was approved and ratified in September 2012.

1.2 Why Instagram marketing is key to eCommerce success?

We all know how great Instagram is to share photos and videos with friends and family, but it's also a fantastic eCommerce marketing channel. But why?

Well, the format of Instagram is an apparent reason. Because of this visual nature, Instagram Holds enormous opportunities for e-commerce companies looking to highlight their goods. Whether through regular pictures, videos, or Instagram stories, millions of businesses have learned that building a visual presence on Instagram can much compliment their marketing on eCommerce.

Instagram users are also more engaged than the average user of social media. And while statistics appear to show that interaction with Instagram is dropping, the site still delivers higher engagement levels for companies relative to both Twitter and Facebook.

But users of Instagram are more than just engaged — they are often online shoppers as well. According to a survey, 72% of Instagram users report making a purchase decision after seeing something on Instagram, with the most common categories being clothes, hair, accessories, and jewelry.

This shopping mentality makes Instagram users the perfect audience because they're high-intent and quick to convert.

Another reason that Instagram platform is so great for eCommerce is that Instagram recently introduced a ton of new business-facing tools, and there's more to come! Whether through Instagram Stories links or Instagram shopping posts, many of our online shopping experiences will start (and end) on Instagram as soon as possible.

All this said, it would be a mistake to think that your business doesn't belong on Instagram just because you don't sell eCommerce products! Instagram is also an incredible place for brands to create brand awareness and communicate with new audiences (and potential customers) in addition to its remarkable ability to move goods.

If you want to create a marketing strategy that resonates with your target audience, you need first to grasp how the Instagram algorithm operates.

1.3 The Instagram algorithm

As Instagram first revealed substitution of the sequential stream with an algorithm in 2016, many people responded with a less than positive reaction. And since then, not much has improved.

So why did Instagram make the change from algorithm to chronological?

Well, it was all about size. As the popularity of Instagram grew, it became harder to keep up with all the sharing of photos and videos. In reality, according to Instagram, when it was linear, people missed an average of 70% of their feeds.

In spite of this, Instagram developed an algorithm that reorganized feeds for users to see more material that was important to them technically.

It also had certain unwanted effects, sadly.

While a linear feed needs little-to-none guesswork (all you have to think about is publishing while your audience is most active), a lot of different factors will affect algorithm-based feeds— such as how much attention a post receives or how long people spend reading your comments.

Instagram is constantly updating the algorithm to boost user experience and promote those types of content; it can be difficult to know. Customize the posts to get as much attention as possible and hit them. But that's not impossible!

Last year, Instagram actually recorded how the Instagram algorithm operates, including factors that determine how the Instagram algorithm will execute the post (and how many people will see it!). Here they are below, ranked in importance as follows:

1: Interest, Instagram is predicting how much you are going to care about a post.

The higher it shows in your list, the more they hope you'll "want" the comment. According to Instagram, this is focused on "past behavior on similar content and possibly machine vision that analyzes the actual post material."

Thought of this one like the Instagram Discover site: if you like a slime clip, the whole discovery page is full of slime clips. And if someone posts a video of slime in your feed, Instagram will guess you're going to like that too.

2: Timeliness, how long have you been sharing a photo or video?

Recent posts will be prioritized by the new Instagram algorithm, so hopefully, you will see fewer posts from over a week ago.

While the feed does not, by any means, go back to chronological, Instagram is beginning to care much more about when you post, rather than just the content or engagement on the post.

This was verified at the end of 2017 after Instagram promised not to reveal older posts on updates of users.

3: Partnership

Businesses need to be more conscious of when their use is most interested in Instagram so that they can schedule their content to show at the moment.

How do you know about your feed's accounts? When you regularly post on the photographs of someone or get associated with them in pictures, it indicates to Instagram that they fall into the category of "friends and family." As a result, you'll probably see more content posted by them (and vice versa!).

To companies, this is great news because it offers them a way to remain top-of-list. Just request your followers to tag you in their posts and make sure you optimize your posts and stories on Instagram to get as many comments as you can.

4: Speed how often do you launch the Instagram application?

If you're a regular scroller, your stream will appear "chronological" because Instagram is attempting to "display you the best posts since your last trip."

5: Unless you update the Instagram app less often,

Then your feed will be filtered more to what Instagram feels you're going to like, rather than chronologically.

How many people on Instagram are you following? If you are following a lot of people, then there are more options for Instagram to choose from, so you hopefully won't see all the posts from each account.

6: Use if you're spending a lot of time on Instagram

You'll see more updates because Instagram "digs further into its archive." If you're spending only a few minutes every day on the site, you'll get the highlights from the algorithm.

1.4 Identifying your goals and objectives

Now that we've discussed how the Instagram algorithm operates, let's think about establishing goals and objectives for your Instagram advertising.

For example, the first move on Instagram to describe your ambitions and objectives is to understand exactly what "performance" means for you.

Create brand awareness and meet more of your potential consumers use Instagram? To introduce your products and services? To create a group that is engaged? Is Will increasing the value of the brand?

Will you be using Instagram as a customer service tool? Can you depend on it to teach your market or industry followers?

When it comes to using Instagram to achieve your business goals, there are plenty of options, and how you use it is ultimately up to you. Just keep in mind that the targets you set will have a major impact on the measures you use to measure your Instagram progress.

For example, if you use Instagram to build a large and engaged audience, you are more likely to focus on metrics of engagement, such as likes, comments, and shares.

If you have trouble deciding on your account's priorities, the following questions can be considered:

• Why are you using Instagram?

• How can Instagram help you achieve your marketing objectives?

- How much time or money can you spend on Instagram?

- How do you get anything special from other sites from Instagram?

1.5 How to create an Instagram business account?

Online viewers are used from every angle to have advertisements and material aimed at them. A busy stream for social media is beginning to look like an endless blur of scattered news. Fortunately, with visuals that tell a story in a moment, you can break through this fog of content.

Before exploring it further, customers must SEE your value proposition. The good news is people who are more open to a call-to-action to follow your content. In fact, after having liked a post on Instagram, 75 percent of users take action, such as visiting a website, shopping, or searching online.

It's easy to learn how to set up Instagram for business, mainly if you already use Facebook. Instagram is more straightforward and less time-consuming than other sites from a business point of view.

You can use visual micro-stories to find out what's entertaining your audience and grow a following quickly. Take these steps to create a profile on Instagram and start promoting your business.

1. Download the App

Continue installing the app if you've never used Instagram. Instagram is available via the Applies, Google Play, and Windows app stores for smartphones, tablets, and computers.

The app hashtag towards mobile devices, and for most of your posting activity, you are likely to use a smartphone or tablet.

If those choices work better for you, you can visit the Instagram website or use the app on a desktop computer.

2. Build an Account

Start the app and create an account in one of two ways:

- Option 1: Register with your email addresses or phone number and enter a username afterward.

- Option 2: You can sign in with the same data and connect the accounts if you have a Facebook account.

Have an account already? Sign in and go directly to your profile page.

3. Connect to Facebook

You start with a personal profile by default. You need to connect your account to a Facebook business page to use Instagram for business purposes. At the bottom of the screen, click on the profile icon.

Open the settings menu at the top right corner of the page. It appears as an Android vertical ellipse or an iOS device.

Scroll down to "Turn to Business Profile" on the next page until you see "Return to Business Profile." Click the slideshow to get a prompt to link to Facebook. Set the site to "open" and select "Choose a profile." Click, "OK." First, Instagram demands permission to monitor the Facebook pages. Look through the list of business pages that you have already created on Facebook. Select the right page and click "Next." An admin can only complete this step on the account. If you're only an authorized user, you won't see the page.

4. Complete the Profile Setup

To complete your profile, enter your business email, telephone number, and address. To proceed, you must fill in at least one of these contact fields. If it already exists on your Facebook page, some details will be auto-filled.

Click the "Done" button and go to your profile. At the top of the Instagram app, a new graph icon will appear. This is your Insights page that allows you to keep track of promotions and stats of engagement.

You can return to the profile page at any time and switch back to a personal account.

5. Create a New Business Page

You can do this at the same time if you have not already created a Facebook business page. Select "Build one" at the bottom of the screen when you get the option to select a page.

Set a page title and pick the class that best describes your company. Some choices include:

- Books and magazines

- Products and services

- Music

- Sports

- Sources of events

- Local businesses

- Websites and forums choose a subcategory to help people find their search page.

For instance, if you used "local businesses" as a subcategory, you've got options like the bar, home improvement, or arts and entertainment. Click the "Next" button. Go back to your profile and click on "Edit your profile." You can add a link to your photo, bio, and website here. When switching from a personal account, consider changing your image, name, and username to represent your company. Using the logo and business name of your brand makes it easier for customers on Instagram to find you. If you don't have a design yet, you can make a logo in minutes.

1.6 Build a consistent Instagram aesthetic

One of the hardest things to do to make your Instagram feed look amazing is to figure out how to make all your photos look good next to each other.

Take a step back from posting a photo to look at your whole Instagram feed: how do all your pictures go together? Here are a few tips.

1: Choose a color scheme: which is important for your Instagram feed to have a consistent color scheme. This means is that all of your feed's colors go together seamlessly. This could be a warm and cozy feed, a dark and cool feed, or a bright and colorful feed. Whatever direction you take, it's a great way to incorporate your branding into your Instagram feed.

2: Lighting emphasis: is a key element in healing and beauty. Think of a magazine you love to read. Regardless of the subject matter, the lighting and color choices are what binds it together and make a theme. The quality of these decisions is the foundation for your Instagram aesthetic.

3: Spread Out Your Content: This is probably the hardest part to create a stunning Instagram aesthetic. You need to learn where to place each of your pictures and how to arrange your stream in order to tie everything together.

The goal is to create a field depth close to what you'd like in photography. Essentially, you want to arrange busy pictures with a combination of simpler or sparse pictures to create a good balance.

4: Keep Things Clear: To help keep your stream running smoothly, you need a consistent approach to editing your pictures. This does not mean you only have to select one plug-in and one filter, but it will help you adhere to your desired style by restricting yourself to a few.

Did you prefer cooler tones? Cooler pictures? Whatever your style of editing, make sure it's consistent so that your posts flow through your feed. Even adding a touch of the same filter each time you post can make your brand and Instagram feed seem more cohesive.

5: Cure with User-Generated Content (UGC): While more businesses invest in original content than ever before, it is still so much to be achieved from incorporating user-generated content (UGC) into your Instagram strategy.

Keep in mind that it is important to stay aligned with your theme and aesthetic when selecting photos to repost to your account. You'll want to choose natural match images with a similar color scheme and style of editing to your own feed. When someone looks at your Instagram feed, it's not meant to be too clear which images are yours and which photos are UGC you've selected.

The most important rule to use is to always ask for permission before reposting the image of someone else on Instagram. And you always want to refer to the original photographer in the caption when you give credit. It's not enough just to mark them in the picture.

1.7 Why do you use Instagram to market?

Let's start with the basics on our way to making you a master. What's advertising for Instagram, and how can you use it for your business?

As one of the most common marketing channels of today, the network provides you with a broad range of ways to reap its advantages. All you need is a good strategy and a commitment to do it.

Instagram Marketing Description Advertising Instagram is a type of social media marketing in which advertisers use the Instagram platform to promote their companies. If "promoting their business" sounds wide, that's because it's: Instagram marketing can involve several different strategies and tactics that can be used to achieve all sorts of goals that a business might have.

When you look at different methods of using Instagram for ads, you can split the practice into two main categories: paying strategies such as advertisement and influencer marketing unpaid techniques such as generating organic content, such as posts, Instagram articles, and tweets, as well as interacting with other users' content.

We're going to get into the particulars of how to create targets and how to use those tactics to achieve them a little ago.

You may have heard the term "algorithm," which is a concept that is widely misunderstood. You don't need to be an Instagram algorithm master, but a basic understanding of it can help you attain your objectives more efficiently and with fewer headaches.

While some advertisers fear their arch enemy is the Instagram algorithm, it's a buddy. That's because, like any other online algorithm, its ultimate goal is to deliver relevant, entertaining, and engaging content to each user.

Algorithms do this by studying the activities and behaviors of their users carefully, then using this data to make informed guesses about what those users will want to see in the future. If the "test" passes your content, you're teed up for success.

Instagram is a staple of marketing campaigns for many small businesses. And that's why. It has a broad and diverse audience that is delighted to connect with brands, resulting in overall high commitment.

Such advantages have been demonstrated by analysis and case studies, showing that they can directly translate into revenue and lead.

Consider this:

- 80% of users follow and use at least one brand on Instagram, with the majority of these users saying they have discovered new products or services via the platform.

- At least 30% of Instagram users bought products that they found on Instagram.

- 65% of Instagram's top-performing posts specifically highlight items.

People are happy to follow brands, and on the site linked my Instagram, they are continually finding and buying products. That's a great victory.

Therefore, worth mentioning is the recent efforts of Instagram to promote exchange.

Ads on Instagram have excellent results and offer a high level of commitment. Instagram shopping streamlines the process of Instagram sales. And company profiles with more than 10,000 followers from Instagram receive "Swipe Up" links that they can attach to Instagram Stories to drive traffic directly to the site, something that was previously hard to do on the website.

• The platform continues to expand, making it more valuable for merchants and e-commerce companies, particularly if they have substantial clickable hashtag items. Only by entering #and then the desired phrase, as you would on a post, can these be added to your profile description now. It's the right choice for most companies to rely on your branded hashtag.

• Links to profiles that can be clicked. There are several ways to use this, but you can now add clickable links in your own Instagram bio to other user profiles. You can use this to maintain traffic there if you have two different patterns for a sister company. When you host a contest with another merchant, while addressing the competition in your bio, refer to them. If that suits your marketing, you can also use this function to send people to your profile.

• The highlights of the story. A few sections down, we'll talk more about Story Highlights. Still, this relatively new feature allows you to add "expired" accounts to different featured categories, which will be displayed on your profile above your Instagram feed. It makes your profile look fleshed out and allows you to view some main Instagram content, such as UGC or posts that illustrate the story of your brand.

There are several ways you use to get results from, each of which will benefit your business in different ways.

1. Share content created by your community. You can use Stories to share user-generated content that is always a crowd-pleaser. Your followers of Instagram love to see that you care about them and their content enough to feature them on your site. It also prevents you from having to create your content and serves as compelling social proof.

2. Also, collecting stories from your audience Stories will help you get UGC, which can happen in various ways. For users to share images of their latest purchase, you can put calls to action. You can also use survey stickers to receive feedback and provide immediate social evidence.

3. Share moments from events Your Stories is also a great place to cover up and encourage activities, whether they are a

couple of weeks away, happening right now, or from the past. It is a perfect way to provoke FOMO to remind everyone what they want, which can boost brand awareness and attendance.

4. Be an authentic Instagram story are more bizarre than feed content, so it's a great place to display your fun side. Using images and videos to tell the story of your brand and, if possible, add in some content behind the scenes.

5. Go live Instagram stories allow you and your fans to broadcast live from your mobile phone.

1.8 Role of Instagram as a marketing platform

Instagram is a forum that e-commerce companies can incorporate if they have not already applied to their advertising roster. Embrace it entirely by actively immersing yourself in the various features, regularly posting different types of content, and engaging your audience. You may even be shocked at the pace at which you see the results coming in.

INFLUENCER MARKETING HAS BECOME A HOT TOPIC on the lips of many marketers, and it is not difficult to understand why when you think about the potential.

With a community of over 600 million active users, including many incredible content creators, Instagram has become a top visual marketing platform for businesses of all kinds— start-ups as well as huge global brands.

Instagram's new algorithm change (posts are now viewed based on communication rather than chronological order) means paid ads, and influencer marketing has just become more relevant than ever.

What is marketing influencer?

The marketing of influencers is not a new phenomenon. It is based on word-of-mouth recommendations. Social media have revitalized the influence of this marketing technique.

Brands can use influencer marketing to partner with a specific social influencer, tapping into their imagination and engaging the audience to create brand awareness authentically and naturally.

When a friend suggests a holiday destination, it's not much different. You value their feedback because you have faith in their judgment. Marketing influencer works the same way, allowing you to target an audience of like-minded people who follow a trusted influencer.

Who are the influencers?

One of Instagram's most exciting aspects of influencer marketing is the fantastic mix of people represented from the entire world, covering all kinds of niches.

Personal trainers use Instagram to share their workouts, fashion bloggers to show off their style, interior designers to show off their portfolio, photographers traveling to document their experiences, and even chefs posting their recipes.

While some of these influencers exceed those of traditional celebrities with follower counts, they are viewed quite differently. Life will often feel more related to an influencer. When they decide to work with a company, their opinion is not only real, but their followers will also take it more seriously.

Influencer marketing in 5 phases it can take time to find an influencer and to work with them. An exercise that's difficult to scale. For best results, use this five-step process to stay on track.

1. Do your homework.

You can learn so much from other brands. Find out what works for them, gain inspiration from the different content styles they share, and see what content types get the most engagement.

Looking at what others are doing is a prominent place to start your research. We use our Whaler Labs tool to enable you to see indicators on your Instagram account and then make comparisons with up to three others. Researching other products, which are not your competitors, but maybe share a similar demographic, is also a good idea. We keep an eye on what Herschel is doing at Shore Projects as we feel that a Herschel customer is also likely to be a customer of Shore Projects.

If there's a story behind your brand, research that as well. Our roots come from the Uk seaside, and we spend a lot of time keeping an eye on accounts centered on the seaside and nautical.

Finally, Instagram Business Blog is a good reference point. They report case studies regularly and announce new updates and resources. Finding posts directly about how marketers should get the most out of Instagram is a great place.

2. Set a clear brief.

The project will be more effective if you encourage the creative freedom influencer to produce content; they know they would enjoy their audience. While criticizing a brief with the goals you want to achieve is equally important, allowing creative freedom is one of the key methods to make Instagram successful in influencer marketing. Rather than giving the exact image, title, and every last hashtag they need to use, it is better to trust them to build an accurate and interactive campaign for you.

A mood board is one report that you could provide a summary. Photos of mood boards where we exchange shore thoughts are shown below. We are helping to give influencers a sense of the general aesthetic appeal we like.

3. Select influencers that are important.

When you have a clear knowledge of what you want to accomplish, identifying relevant influencers is the next vital step. It can be challenging to get this wrong, so it is worth investing a little more time to make the right decision.

Mostly, there are influencers in every market. Whether it's fashion, lifestyle, travel, wellness, more than a few good options are likely to be found. One of the methods to find people is by searching your market for the top Instagram hashtags and looking for highly engaging posts (lots of likes and comments). You can also discover influencers on other brands' accounts quite often. Look for positions where someone else is tagged as the creator of content.

Finding specific influencers can be quite tricky without spending a long time trawling through hundreds of Instagram accounts, where resources like Whaler come into play. You may search for an influencer list by topic, place, interaction, prices, etc. — all of which are interested in working with related brands.

4. Agree on a framework of cooperation.

You will need to reach out to them and agree on a collaborative structure once you have found the influencers you want to work with. There are usually six key aspects you're going to want to work around: Timeframe–stay up-to-date on the timetable and illustrate the need to reach it.

Output–be clear about what you want to make them. For instance, two pieces of content, one to be published with a mention of your brand on the influencer's page, and one to be used at your discretion. Data Use–Let them know what rights to use the data you use. The influencer will always retain ownership as the author, but we usually ask for a reason for use for two years of the full content.

Payment–For their expertise, almost all of the best influencers would demand a fee. Occasionally, as part of that charge, they may be willing to negotiate or take a free product/service/experience; however, you can expect to make a payment. When negotiating a price, remember to pay for multiple services: content creation, rights of use, and access to their audience.

Sponsored Hashtag –Sponsored content regulations are varied around the world and are continually changing. I recommend a side warning error and use #spoon or #ad at all times. We found that the quality of response to the post makes absolutely no difference.

Aim of the Promotion—Focus specifically on the objective you are trying to achieve while communicating with the influencer. That could be as easy as increasing your profile followers or driving clicks to your website or brand page through your Instagram bio to increase sales. Knowing what you are working towards as the goal of the campaign keeps both of you aligned.

5. Maximize the value of the content.

Get additional value by repurposing it to other platforms from supported Instagram material. Here are three examples of ways for Shore Projects to maximize the content value:

1. Publish it on the product page. To publish the influencer content on your product pages, we use the Shopify Apathies' not only makes our product pages look great, but it also adds positive social proof and has even led to the presentation of their content by real customers.

2. We learned that it is essential to keep your ad units refreshed with new material at a Facebook marketing event. We initially used our photography of brand and lifestyle and found it very difficult to continue creating new graphics all the time.

We can now refresh our ad units regularly by using influencer content. Also, using influencer material, our conversion rate has increased by 19 percent.

3. Publish it on social media. We also share content on our social media accounts generated by influencers. Approximately 80% of the innovative we share on social media accounts on the Shore Projects comes from influencers and real customers.

Please make sure that you are allowed to use the pictures of other people.

Influencer marketing can be a cost-effective way to create highly creative content for your brand, develop brand advocacy, and tap into the engaged audiences of other people.

CHAPTER 2: TEAM ORGANIZATION

Developing the perfect Instagram marketing squad is very much like creating a sports team. Each player (or marketer) has a list of unique gifts and talents to bring to the table, but what makes the team outstanding is their ability to work together towards a common goal.

Every day, digital marketing becomes more complicated, making it harder than ever before for this dream team to be brought together. Nonetheless, you will find better talent with the right tools and plans in place to pull together a stronger group that is looking towards change and growth.

It's going to get you nowhere to suggest a team structure without top-to-bottom assistance. You want to make sure they look good because the organization's confidence is in the superiors. There has to be planned a detailed review, and no rocks left unturned.

Consider what your future grievances need to suggest. The more relaxed you are, more the likelihood of a good option.

Start with the picture of the perfect marketing team and work backward. Start and move forward with the success-based first candidate. Creating an entire digital marketing squad is no small feat.

After all, the superhero team plays an enormous role in your company's failure or success. The need for digital marketing resources is high, yet less than half of the job market openings are the talent pool of today.

To push the company on a positive track, you need to build an approach and find the right group of outstanding Instagram marketers.

Here are the three movements that you need to follow to find the right marketing team leaders to prepare the campaign that will waste so much time.

2.1 Defining your ideal team

You must first describe what you're searching for when you are looking for recruits. Despite not having to work out everything, you should understand what kind of expertise is needed for an effective marketing campaign.

Keep in mind that Instagram's advertising environment is evolving daily and declining rivalry and more traditional skills. According to McKinley's marketing hiring trends study, there is an exponential increase in demand for creative skills such as design and copywriting, as well as expertise in digital advertising and content curation.

While planning the perfect marketing campaign is ultimately up to this group, you may already have an idea of what strategies you'd like to use.

Are you going to focus on marketing content? Then you will find a good content creator and a photographer.

Want to maximize the SEO nail down?

Looking for someone with a good history of SEO, communicating building experience, etc. Once you grasp it, you will be able to pursue marketers with additional skills that might be useful along the way.

We were responsible for addressing multiple departmental needs— and often, a significant challenge is prioritization.

The project manager connects the department of digital marketing with the rest of the company. Part of this role involves personnel management, while the other part manages new requests from followers, meaning that everyone gets what they need.

Strategists Impactful marketing starts with a good plan and a strong understanding of who your followers are and what matters most to them.

But while the group produces content and embraces projects, it is possible to lose sight of higher marketing and business priorities. Therefore, that important is a policy.

- Your strategist is responsible for:

- Identifying buyers

- Mapping customer journey

- Understanding keyword opportunities

- Establishing key success metrics

- Ensuring that all marketing activities align with broader business objectives

- Measuring and optimizing performance content

Your strategist serves as a brand editor, ensuring that all published strategic boxes are checked in full.

Content writer, when you don't have someone to create your content, all your marketing planning, and brilliant ideas won't make a difference.

It's best to find a diverse writer who can create all sorts of content outlined in your content marketing strategy, including

- Blogs

- Website content

- Automated email copy

- Sell sheets

- Gated pieces like eBooks and white papers.

Graphic designer Striking visual characteristics are no longer a' good thing to have. They are integral to your product and essential for digital noise. Visuals make it easier for viewers to understand the message than just text.

Every product you're building should have an element of design. While using stock pictures can help you getaway, you'll need a skilled graphic designer if you want custom-designed components. Use a freelancer or an independent development agency if you're aiming for a single project such as an eBook or infographic. Make sure you're as comprehensive as a product author if you're heading this path.

SEO specialist, it is unlikely that your content will be found in a search. Many people don't go through the results page of the first search. That's why web success is crucial to SEO.

The SEO expert is supposed to love Google Analytics and learn the SEO software you're using. We use free tools such as Google Analytics and the Search Console at Brand point, plus paying apps such as SEMrush and Spy Fu to help keep an eye on the SEO pulse.

Your SEO expert ensures that all digital content is tailored to scan, upgrade things such as headlines, alt-text photo, and optimal metadata rating. You also have to own and review the

SEO and keyword strategy and perform SEO reviews to find material that needs optimization.

Ideally, everybody should be an SEO professional at some point in a digital marketing department, but getting a specialist can be a great asset.

Product creation and advertisement are a critical element of growth in almost all promotional fields. In driving traffic and growing viewers, resources such as out brain and AdWords are crucial.

They also need to monitor, update, test, and optimize a lot. It is perfect for getting someone who is dedicated to this role, whether you do it in-house or have an outsourced worker.

Although this may seem like a "good to have" function, it may be an incredibly useful tool for a front-end developer.

Front-end programmers are experts in calling for action, building landing pages, incorporating structured data, and planning and implementing whatever forms of pop-ups you may want to use. You will learn as you go if you have active CMS like WordPress and useful templates. But for a talented artist, most marketing tools are quick, easy.

Expert in marketing automation Great email marketing and marketing automation can be massive undertakings, involving:

- Database management

- Advanced consumer segmentation

- Robust interaction and lead scoring strategies if you use either email marketing or marketing automation, you know that it is certainly sufficient to keep one person occupied, so it helps to have someone in charge. Other responsibilities can undoubtedly be shared among others on the team, such as creating emails.

Social media boss, you need a social media manager right there if the team is active on social media.

Social media is not just a place where people share the silly GIFs and photos of their child connecting with customers on a personal level, your company can use your content (and some filtered content).

It is a network of high-stake customer service. When people don't like your online customer service, some of your existing customers might be driven away.

One of the best loyalty tools could be a customer-and audience-centric media strategist.

2.2 Successfully merging tasks

How to successfully merge tasks while these are both essential duties and obligations of an Instagram marketing department, in each of these positions, no organizations have the assets or the need for dedicated people.

Based on your marketing team's scope and capabilities, decide how to combine two or more of these tasks to ensure that you have a comprehensive approach to your Instagram marketing activities.

For example, the producer of your content may be an excellent social media and group administrator. He has an intimate relationship with the material itself and a deep understanding of who the audience is and what they value.

You might also be a perfect strategist for your project manager. She is profoundly in touch with the follower's expectations, as well as the sales team's overall business goals. She understands the demand of followers and can support the rest of the team to turn that into a good content strategy.

Only think about the talents of the people in your marketing team and how they fit with the desires and responsibilities of each role to successfully integrate both tasks.

Seasoned talent can spot a mile away a structure of an unorganized company, so you need to have a plan before you get on a team.

Investing in the right tools such as technology for project management and communication systems may mean the difference between campaign success and failure, particularly while building a team from scratch.

Studies have concluded that companies that use these types of management programs can raise their project success rates to 88% and spend 28 times less money than their competitors.

New units will have to learn how to stay connected and work on projects together.

This process can be made much more comfortable by a task management tool with shared calendars and assignment portals. Talent and knowledge will only go so far if the right tools and processes are not in place for your team to keep things running smoothly. You need to have a rock-solid system in place first if you want to recruit the best squad.

With this task, the person who assigned you is the key to your success. Make sure you keep them updated throughout the process of your results.

Do not wait until the end to discuss with your donor your decision. When you show your results to them without background, their needs will not be fulfilled.

With your partner, early check-in lets you fine-tune the decision. And as a bonus, it will help them believe more in your strategy!

Remember: you're not going to sell the project to the company on your own.

Recommending a team structure without endorsement from top to bottom is likely to get you nowhere.

CHAPTER 3: STEPPING IN

3.1 Breaking down your platform barriers

This seems obvious, but you must be sure that your profile is complete.

You want to be as trustworthy as possible. That also means filling out the fearful "About Me" section.

And make sure you add a link to your website in your bio. (Image Source) You must also connect your Instagram account to your Facebook account.

Decide whether you want to associate your Instagram with a personal or corporate Facebook, or make a page for Instagram's sole purpose.

It depends on you, but if your company's Facebook page already has connections, it's likely wise to link your Instagram for maximum exposure.

It is an idea to ensure that all the images still follow a similar pattern.

For businesses looking to use Instagram, the platform may seem more complicated than worth it by barriers: finding content, integrating Instagram into their social strategy, and scheduling.

Most companies feel that they don't have enough image-based content to use Instagram for business effectively. You undoubtedly did not take the photos in your set with Instagram in mind. Using Instagram to make sure you spend hours choosing lovely pictures, manually uploading them to your desktop, and writing a custom message with a small phone keyboard.

Good news: this is not the only response to the original content. Data curation operates on Instagram as well as in other networks. It is fiddly on phone apps that ease the data recovery process by searching and using high-quality visual content from multiple sources.

These applications make searching easy and comfortable to share excellent materials from Instagram, Facebook, Pinterest, blogs, or collections of Unlash and Pickaway (using a Smarter Queue bookmark or extension). And you may need to link a photo archive to your own media set.

In addition to breaking specific platform barriers, Instagram applies a strategy to connect to other business accounts across social media such as Facebook on Twitter, etc. By linking your stories to other social apps in a way that makes them more realistic, you can connect to your business pages and support each other.

Because it is a widely available tactic to market your products and allow your customer's easy access. Therefore, Instagram works extensively with Facebook and Twitter to make them user-friendly and linked to better networks and save time. By following these fundamental steps

1. Go to your account and click your name.

2. Tap Settings. Tap Settings.

3. Tap Account > Accounts linked, and then choose Facebook

4. If you haven't, enter your login information on Facebook.

5. Your Instagram account will share your Facebook profile by default. To share a page, pick a page that you control below

3.2 Targeting the audience

Instagram quickly stormed the social media world. To over 300 million people posting over 70 million photos and videos each day, Instagram has evolved from a network of close friends sharing photos to a massive product and company ecosystem sharing experiences and telling stories as they happen.

Like popular peer networks, Instagram gradually added ads to the mix. Too early adopters ' dismay, the ad-free feed days are gone. But that doesn't mean you have to move on the paid social sites to make a business out of Instagram. At least not yet.

One thing remained the same. Instagram is a gem of visual discovery.

Here are opportunities to discover and reach the target audience on the old-fashioned way–absolutely ad-free.

1. Target audiences and hashtag networks Hashtags were a key application discovery tool from day one. In June, the network boosted hashtag discovery with a new one to make discovery "immediate and effortless." Identify and use popular hashtags to gain visibility among your target audience. Finding the right tags will take some work, but using the most important and commonly utilized will get the best results. A few ways: find competitors along with peer organizations and check what they use.

Use Instagram's search feature–key terms and phrases plug-in, and go from there. Often one hash tag leads to the next.

Identify active target users. Use tags relevant to you and what you're about?

Most small communities utilize hashtags within the international Instagram culture. If you find them, they're gold. For example, Maine has an active photo community. #igersmine hashtag would be a great way for a location or venue to gain visibility. A more international focused hashtag instance might be #dogsofinstagram. This would suit a dealer that sells dog toys and accessories.

2. The best way to engage the already busy Instagram community is to interact directly with your peers and target audience through @mentions. Identify famous accounts already followed by your community and @mention them important and credible. Chances of reposting your post to their followers are pretty good. Boom–you just reached your target audience, deepening your community roots. Rinse, repeat.

3. Add the location context along with the brand location tag If there is a social aspect to your business and the photos being shared; be sure to tag them with a location. Tag photos taken on your site to enhance the link between the content and your brand name when they get extra exposure and play in popular hashtag feeds. Tag photos taken at popular locations to increase your exposure to users who are browsing memories and events captured in specific areas.

There are three easy-to-execute strategies to develop the following Instagram and improve interaction. Of course, as with any marketing effort, you should be influenced by a social media strategy. Keep tabs on how and what's going on. Check out my favorite Instagram analytical tools, Icon square.

Despite the addition of ads, Instagram's brilliant star appeal remains—real-time news feed that allows 100% organic reach, no restrictive news feed algorithm... yet. We'll see if the parent of the Facebook-owned network is the way it is. For now, let's enjoy the possibilities of reach and exposure.

Having an in-depth knowledge of your Instagram target audience is a key part of a successful Instagram marketing strategy.

On Instagram and get to know the best Instagram targeting tactics to reach them. This post will help you do exactly that.

Start with larger people the idea of what the typical customer looks like for in your business. Ask yourself what your product is like and what it's about. Who is your product for? What's your audience looking for?

A product like Ever note, for egg, makes it easier for people to take notes and organize the relevant information.

As a result, their target audience would typically be: busy professionals, looking for solutions to organize their information and increase their productivity.

4. Collect competitive insights You can learn a lot about your target audience by looking at the Instagram audience of your competitors. See what kind of followers they've got and what kind of posts they're publishing. This can give you some idea of your target audience on Instagram should look like. this will figure out if there are any gaps or missing segments of the audience that you left out when you started putting together a picture of your audience.

Just entering their social media handle, and the device will generate a comprehensive audit report of their accounts.

You can discover essential audience insights, such as their locations of followers, demographics, and brand citations.

5. Use existing demographic data Current demographic ideas that you can get from your Instagram analytics which can guide you a lot about your Instagram target audience.

Go to "Audience" under "Insights." in this, you can see some vital statistics about your current followers, including their age, gender, and location along with other specifications.

Combine this data with your buyer and the information you collected from competition research. This is supposed to help you paint a clear picture of what your Instagram target audience looks like.

6. Active listening to meaningful conversations Audience research is one of the first steps in recognizing and successfully reaching the audience.

One of the ways to understand your Instagram target audience is by listening socially. If you do not know what your audience is thinking about and what they are interested in, you would find it difficult to understand how to reach them.

Use Sprout Social's social media listening tools to identify conversations in your industry and on specific topics. This gives you an insight into what your target audience is talking about, how they feel about a specific subject, and who drives these conversations

7. Connect to right influencers Specific niches are the direct result of the passion and expertise of influencers. They gathered hundreds of thousands of followers whose interests match their niche.

So, it can be highly effective to partner with the right players to reach your Instagram target audience. This would entail a relationship between the target audience and influencers.

There are a few ways to find suitable Instagram influencers for your brand.

3.3 Serving up exclusive content

What are the best images and videos on Instagram?

If you want Instagram performance, you need to learn which kinds of posts perform well. While each audience is different, fortunately, a lot of data has been compiled to give us some insight into where to start.

They're relatively open in terms of the types of posts that people want to see. They are happy to see promotional posts, motivational quotes, product photos, content for DIY or tutorials, and images shared by other users (i.e., content generated by users). That being said, they want to see variety; if you use one type of post for too long, they're going to get bored or annoyed.

such Videos can share more information with users, making them valuable, but usually, high-quality photos get an average 36 percent higher commitment. If you're using Instagram video, keep it short; Instagram users are mainly mobile users, and they're unlikely to hang around for more than 10 to 15 seconds at a time.

You should also adjust the different camera effects because by using Boomerang for every single post, you don't want to give users a migraine.

The esthetics of images and videos are much more relevant in many respects. After all, Instagram is a visual-centered platform.

Here's what we learn about the imagery that performs best on Instagram, thanks in large part to a Correlate study:

• Lighter photographs presented better than darker ones• More backdrop or white space are favored

• Photographs with bluer dominant colors improved over dominant red colors, and pictures with a single dominant color worked better than those with multiple dominant colors

• Pictures with contrasting colors. Share content created by your audience

You can use Stories to display content generated by users, which is always a crowd-pleaser. Your fans on Instagram want to see that you care about them and their posts enough to feature them on your page. It also saves you from creating the content on your own and acts as power collecting stories from your viewer Stories will help you receive UGC, which can happen in various ways. For users to share photos of their purchase, you can place calls to action. You can also use poll stickers to receive feedback and provide immediate social evidence. Share moments from events Your Stories is also a great place to cover up and promote events, whether they are a couple of weeks away, happening right now, or from the past. This is a perfect way to provoke FOMO to remind everyone what they want, which can boost brand awareness and participation. Be authentic Instagram stories is more bizarre than feed content, so it's a great place to display your fun side. Using images and videos to tell the story of your company and, if necessary, add in some material behind the scenes. Go live Instagram Stories enables you to broadcast live from your mobile phone right away, and your followers can engage in real-time. You may hold Quash, explore a particular topic, or interview a guest or influencer featured. You can have it set to play with the rest of your stories once they live over.

Serve up Exclusive Content As outlined in Maslow's hierarchy of needs, people have an inherent desire to feel a sense of belonging, be it love, friendship, or acceptance in a group.

This will encourage followers to act. This will motivate them on Instagram to engage with you Offering special discounts when you are about to reward followers with Instagram-exclusive discounts, a few things happen: First, you increase your brand's exposure as followers use word-of-mouth to spread your brand name to family and friends, thereby encouraging them to become your followers.

Most specifically, you are building a relationship that guarantees the return of followers.

Exclusively to Instagram followers, Emily Ley holds regular flash sales promising savings on certain products.

It helps their fans feel like they have a shot most people don't have.

Provide sneak peeks offer another chance to make your followers feel exclusive.

Only demonstrate an item to your customers before it hits the market. Doing so builds the product's excitement, publicity, and desire. On the launch of the drug, people will rush to shop, creating additional excitement. Additionally, you might look behind the scenes of the company's everyday life. Humanizes your brand and creates an emotional connection for followers. It also builds trust because supporters believe that they are part of a community that is genuine and trustworthy.

Form stack needs to know that its followers are not just some mysterious device for form-building. Instead, they are actual people with similar preferences because you maintain a consistent and regular update schedule as one of the most important parts of Instagram advertising. While a lot of social media advertisers realize that keeping a healthy backlog of images is excellent, not all of them recognize that there are ways to make it even simpler to plan content.

Use an app like Later or Buffer to set up the Instagram advertising material schedule. The significant advantage of using such a tool is that you can plan your posts long in advance-including hashtags and captions-which means you, can spend less time on Instagram every day worrying about what to post. You will have more time to interact with your fans and followers, strengthening your social media presence.

People retain only about 10 percent of the information they hear, but this number jumps to 65 percent when paired with a relevant image. You want people to stick to your post. Photos and videos are powerful tools for advertisers to connect with followers effectively.

Nearly every major social network, including Facebook, Instagram, Twitter, and Pinterest, has been taken over by visual content. In reality, videos with related photos, without them, get 94 percent more views than material.

Not only can you increase engagement by adding an image to your social media posts, it can also help you tell a story. Interactive advertising will effectively distill complicated information and help marketers with effect and passion for telling stories rapidly. Tapping in emotions can drive deeper engagement, so make sure you align the visuals you use with your broader goals. In other words, make sure that the images or videos that you use are relevant and are not there to take up space.

It is challenging to come up with original visual content for every post you publish on social media. Luckily there's help. To help your content, we have put together a list of free photo creation tools.

3.4 Using editing apps

Being honest: it's no big secret to use editing tools. VSCO, Enlighten, stuff-you noticed all over or you have purchased a premium version of it?

We've come across a lot of features in my years of using Instagram that have changed the way we use the site.

Here are two applications which are recently found despite there are many other useful applications also but these being completely invaluable:

Snapseed: although it looks very identical to the other editing apps out there, I considered Snapseed (a Google product!) to be the strongest. It has a few power-user capabilities (like a healing brush and curves) that render it the ultimate editing device in addition to an intuitive interface.

Facetune: This is a standard photo editing software. Although it seems to be made for people's pictures, it's cool to touch up photographs and offer them the glitter that is Instagram-friendly.

Huji Cam: Available on iOS and Android Huji Cam have been downloaded more than 16 million times, which is fantastic because the device only does one thing: a low-fi, old school camera filter to make your pictures look retro.

VSCO: iOS and Android VSCO are the first we want to highlight. Today, VSCO is stretching the concept of a stand-alone app— it's a fully functioning enterprise on a considerable growth path! VSCO is raising $50 million per year from app sales and in-app purchases, Wow!

With features, the app itself is tremendously powerful and makes an entirely beautiful experience. You can do almost any kind of photo editing you want: filters, mosaics, you're calling it.

Layout: Free Available on iOS and Android There are plenty of great options when it comes to making collages and multi-photos with layouts for Instagram. One of our favorite picks is Instagram's independent design feature. To build some eye-catching designs, you can merge up to 9 pictures at once.

Carbon is an exclusive black-and-white photo editor to make eye-catching pictures, and effects Facetune is one of the best selfie editors. Facetune's retouching features work like charm! We never felt much more significant.

Bug Art Studio has a lot of different bug effects that you can add to your images.

Darkroom and after light are a few other large and powerful editors of photography, similar to VSCO and Snapseed.

And if you're searching for a quick resizer for Instagram, there are plenty of applications that allow you to resize your picture without cropping. Check for "square and plant"... but check at the ratings because some applications require you go through the hoops to use the device.

3.5 Stepping in the trends

Participating in the right conversations can help you get the right people to notice.

You are using Sprout's online listening software to explore current discussions about your product and your business. This will help you to understand some of the most active conversations on which you can either participate through existing active posts or start new posts with high chances of sparking engagement.

You can also use these tools to track your feelings about your brand and your competitors and understand how people feel about it. This will give an idea of how to differentiate your business and more effectively engage your target audience.

Another explanation is that hashtags will help you get to the Discover site.

If you don't know about Explore page is, click on the explorer icon on your Instagram account on your desktop to see it now. You can find the image in the top right are this page shows trending Instagram posts you may want based on your past activity. There is a' For You ' section where multi-topic jobs and individual topic sections are shown.

Instagram explorer comprises mostly photos of comics, pets, fitness, and nutrition as I engage in these subjects often with media. Instagram shows topics, as well. I can filter relevant photos when I click on them.

Hash tags are one of the many factors that help the Instagram algorithm find posts (which you might like) for your explorer page. This wants to show posts containing hash tags you've connected with in the past, i.e., hash tags have been applied to other articles you've read, shared, tapped, or posted on.

Therefore, if you find and add relevant hash tags, your post will have a higher likelihood that people will interact with your content will be displayed on the explorer pages.

This is what happens in the shares, posts, presence, and supporters of all those.

So, you have to make it a habit of adding hash tags to every post you post. But you are not supposed to add them randomly. You should take a very strategic approach, adding only those that are very relevant.

And a combination of trendy hash tags and niche-specific hash tags must be your relevant hash tags because you will find it easier to get more exposure to niche hash tags that use fewer people than the popular overused ones.

CHAPTER 4: MAKE MONEY FROM YOUR INSTAGRAM ACCOUNT

You need to make sure that brands want to partner with you if you want to make money through Instagram. This means that you need to continue through your follow-up.

Users with over 100,000 followers have a good chance to find brands that are partnering with them. But even if you have a thousand followers, you might still be able to work with brands that need micro-influencers. Use these tips to increase the platform's following: develop high-quality content that would appeal to people in your niche. Make sure that all images are vivid and relevant to the products you want to promote, whether they are products of beauty, fitness products, or clothing.

Using specific hashtags to make it easy for people to discover your content and perhaps even follow you. Tools such as Hashtagify.me will help you find common hashtags that you can use in your posts.

Ask for a shout-out for specific accounts. You can search for a hashtag to find popular Instagram accounts that share content in your niche from different users. Go through their content and get in touch with them to share your post if you notice they're regularly shouting. For example, with more than

180,000 followers, @global. travelz is an Instagram account. If you look through their posts, you will see that they are mostly travel-related photographs that are user-cured. Users of Instagram who want to grow and build a name in the travel niche might ask them to share their content.

Understand how much you should charge

Once you can win several thousand followers for your Instagram account, you need to know how many brands are worth it. This will help you avoid overloading or underloading your customers.

Some influencers might overestimate their value and charge several thousand dollars if they are worth only a few hundred dollars. Others may underestimate their quality and cost just a few hundred dollars for each sponsored post if they could charge more than $1,000.

The Webfluential Influence Estimator is a useful tool to gain a better understanding of how great your posts are. The calculator measures the number of followers and communication rates to see how much to charge per message. Keep in mind that their free tool measures only the price of Twitter. To find out the quality of your Instagram posts, you will need to register as a Webfluential influencer.

You should start looking for brands that will reward you for your Instagram posts after that. If you have millions of followers, you will already have collaboration brands contacting you, so you don't have to read on. But you're going to have to do the grunt work with emerging influencers and search for companies to collaborate with on your own.

The good news is that several influencer networks and advertising channels agree micro-influencers are available. If you are part of this network, you will be contacted by the company with brands that need relevant influencers. Here are a few functional networks and channels for which you can sign up: Buzzweb: if you have more than 5,000 followers, you can join Buzzweband to monetize your impact on Instagram. Based on the size of your following, you can use the app to measure your future monthly earnings. And you can apply for as many projects as you want to be part of. You will be billed within 24 hours after your post has been accepted.

Influence.co: Influence.co spans over 65 + countries to more than 1,000 brands. You can search for those you want to partner with and submit a request to join their campaign directly. If you're still a micro-influencer, it's a lot better than waiting for a company to contact you for a relationship.

TRIBE: TRIBE is an excellent platform for influencers with only a few thousand fans. It's relatively simple to work with brands on the website. All you need to do is search brands you already use and are a fan of. You can then create and submit a post for review for that brand. You will be charged within 48 hours when accepted.

TapInfluence: TapInfluence also exists, which forecasts your monthly earning potential once you have built your profile. You can pick your specific topics and subtopics, then set your level. Then the platform matches you with brands that match your needs.

Fullbottle: Fullbottle would be an ideal platform for you if the content appears to get high levels of interaction. You don't charge per post on this website, but instead, get paid according to your content driving contribution. On the Instagram post, you make for a product, and you can bid a certain amount for any request.

The hardest part to monetize your Instagram account is to increase your follow-up. But the tips will help you overcome this obstacle. And you need to link with the right brands to start earning from Instagram once you have enough followers.

CHAPTER 5: MAINTAINING INSTAGRAM PROFILES

5.1 Visualize a stunning profile

Many merchants know the fundamentals about creating an online profile, you need to fill in your contact details, provide a keyword-optimized overview, and pick a photo identity that is simple to recognize like a logo. This is a great beginning. To continue, you must notify the following basic points.

Get your favorite profiles inspired. Experiment with the colors of the picture. Use the chessboard influence. Change boundaries. Switch borders. Set your profile to the global mood. Using plug-in. Use cookies. Post photos like a net. Using a monitoring profile link. To make a statement, upload multi-grid images. Invest in an efficient visualization tool from Instagram. Concentrate on follower's quality rather than quantity. Build a thoughtful calendar of content. Allow updates to Instagram. Select a suitable handle. Assign a controlling user to the communications channels. To suit the latest campaigns, change your Instagram profile image. Get a blue checkmark to boost credibility. Review your Instagram profile across devices. Ensure you are connecting to a mobile-optimized website. Add emoji for fun.

5.2 Posting high-quality content

Have you ever read an article about one year's top viral posts? If you did, you might have found that most viral messages were visual. This is essentially part of the reduced focus online for people.

Photo, photos, and GIFs are to be generated on social media. These forms of visual content are an essential part of social media, and, if done correctly, it can quickly turn viral. Just begin to record and talk from the heart. That leads to so much more engagement because you usually don't feel like the only one.

More background and/or white space are favored. Pictures with the bluest dominant colors and pictures with a single dominant color have done better than those with multiple dominating color images with a contrasting texture of ten different colors.

5.3 Create a carousel

The "Carousel" feature is the latest update to Instagram's website. Carousel, previously only available to marketers, is an innovative way to spice up your calendar with Instagram material. This is a simple change that enables you to post multiple media items (photos and videos) to a single Instagram post.

While this can certainly be used in a variety of ways, the most exciting applications I found were when the design helped tell a story. It is perfect for displaying a collection of images that create a narrative for viewers because of the way it is laid out. Simple product shots will also do, of course!

5.4 Create a seamless feed

This is one of the favorite unknown secrets of Instagram. Although not for all companies, creating a seamless Instagram feed is a visual spectacle that transforms your profile into a lovely and unique gallery for fans and potential customers. It's like a transparent feed-editing your photos so that your feed looks like a large image.

You will want to use a prototype for your images—you will need a program like Photoshop to edit it in this way. This strategy is excellent for companies that do not rely on the constant creation of content; it is a bit restrictive because every addition to your feed takes a bit more time.

5.5 Create a posting schedule

You should schedule posts on Instagram to see the best results, much like scheduling posts on other social platforms.

Scheduling allows you to post when your audience is most active online, which ensures that your odds during those moments of going viral with a comment are much better.

You will evaluate what those moments are through interaction analysis on the Socialinsight.io platform.

Look at your posting times and then check out the engagement and interaction data. Which times gathered the best likes or comments on posts?

This is when you should be uploading to Instagram.

Then, once you know your optimal post times, schedule posts out in the Socialinsight.io tool to go live at those times and days.

This can be a lot of work, though. Another thing that allows you to go viral is to provide a profile with a broader follow-up.

5.6 Maintain your story

Though Instagram stories are now prevalent, the secret remains how to use them (shameless) appearance of Snapchat best. What's so significant about history is that it's the only way they ensure a position at the top of your follower's lists—as compared to regular posts filtered based on user activity and an Instagram algorithm, the new histories first show.

Although there is no specific set of good practices, here are some common strategies I saw:

• highlight new posts: drawing attention to your latest Instagram posts can draw attention to your profile and increase your participation in your recent competition.

• Run competitions: running a simple contest on your story will involve supporters with your brand and products.

• Highlight promotions: if you have an active deal, highlight it concerning your page on your post.

InstaStories are great for your blog and make you more likely to have viral content.

You can see your profile at the very top of your web feed and go to your page and click on a photo.

This is a great place to demonstrate your wit and humor. However, InstaStories isn't the only place for funny posts.

You can put them on your page correctly.

I don't know about you, but that's the kind of good feeling we like seeing on Instagram.

But once the material is down, make sure that you updated at the right time.

Highlights of the story. Some sections down, we'll talk about history highlights. Still, this relatively new feature allows you to add "expired" accounts to different feature categories that are shown in your profile above your Instagram feed. This makes your profile look sophisticated and allows you to view such essential Instagram material like the UGC or posts that highlight the past of your company.

Historically, expanding the lifetime of stories with highlights will expire after 24 hours, just like the Snapchat feature. Instagram recognized that this led to a loss of ROI and the ability to create highlights.

There are highlights on our profile page, and after 24 hours of glory, we can add stories to them.

The best effect of this is to create multiple highlights with one for user-generated content ("What You Said"), one for brand storytelling ("About Us") and one for events ("Conference 2017"), which makes it easier for users to find content when they reach your profile first, which can help them get to know you a bit more quickly and trust you.

Tap on the black + icon above your gallery to add highlights to your account.

How to Use Instagram Stories for Business

Instagram Business Stories This is where things are beginning to be creative.

Instagram Stories have become an essential element of Instagram marketing strategy since they first arrived on the scene in 2017. Sixty-four percent of businesses are planning to create more Instagram Stories in 2018, according to The State of Instagram Marketing 2018. So, what explains the huge success of Instagram Stories? Okay, this partially has to do with ephemeral video's growing popularity. More businesses are looking forward to the value of creating short-lived video content, whether it's fun and lighthearted or more business-focused. Instagram stories features that are perfect for business when it comes to using Instagram stories as a part of business and Instagram marketing, there are a few features we can use to get the most bang for your buck:

#1: Location and Hashtag Stickers.

Since then, Instagram has added a ton of new features to stickers, including the ability to see location-based stories with the Explore page, and, most recently, its ability to search for stories by location and hashtag. While you were only able to share Instagram Stories with your followers at first, these new features allow anyone to see your Instagram stories!

For example, if you post a story from an Atlanta restaurant, you may mark the place with a sticker, and your story can show in the Instagram stories at that venue. The same applies to hashtag stickers. When a user tags the hashtag in their Instagram stories, it will appear on the corresponding hashtag page.

#2: Recently, Instagram Clickable Links rolled out the ability to add links to Instagram Stories, and it's a pretty big deal. Yes, it is the first time people have ever been able to add a reference to Instagram, which is not the connection in their profile!

For example, it's very convenient to transfer followers from your profiles to different landing pages for Instagram ads. Its functionality can be used to push Instagram traffic to all forms of related landing pages, be it a brand site or a new blog post! TIP: The call for action for' See More,' which is illustrated in stories with references, is quite small and easy to find, so it's a good idea to call it utilizing messages, arrows, and other design features.

#3: Label Other Users They all realize the usefulness of Instagram contests in pushing and getting new followers and in tagging other users in Instagram stories.

#4: Tag Business in your Instagram stories the latest Instagram paying sponsorship feature makes it super easy to get your Instagram stories funded!

So far, only a handful of celebrities, influencers, and companies have been given access to the app, but in the coming months, a larger-scale release is planned.

In general, here, you can find out more about the feature and disclosure.

#5: Polls & Emoji Sliders want to ask your Instagram followers about their preferences, views, dislikes, and more? Okay, you can do it now!

Recently, Instagram launched new social poll stickers on Instagram Stories, which encourage you to ask questions and see responses from your fans as they vote. The great thing about poll stickers has so many business applications!

Whether you want to gather reviews about your items, crowdsource suggestions, or just entertain your fans, poll stickers deliver a completely new way to reach your Instagram community!

Not exactly how to use the company's Instagram Stories polls? Check out our 6 Create Inspiration Ways to Use Instagram Stories Polls!

#6: Question Stickers, poll stickers, and emoji sliders, which allow users to "vote" on questions you submit when you add a question sticker on your Instagram story, other users submit questions for your answers. Whether you want to collect feedback for your products or crowdsource ideas, question stickers offer an entirely new way to engage your Instagram audience!

#7: Countdown Stickers Now, you can add a sticker that is up to date and time if you are posting the forthcoming story (such as in-store selling, product launch, or event). You can then add to your countdown case so that you can give them a reminder when the time has passed.

Whether you wish to promote sales, an event, or something else, it's an excellent method for your followers to share a countdown of your stories.

#8: GIF Stickers Instagram joined forces with GIPHY to build a high-quality GIF library on Instagram Stories in 2017. Now you can add to any photo or video in your story fun, expressive GIF stickers!

It's easy to add GIFs to Instagram Stories — you'll see a new GIF feature when you click to apply a sticker to a photo or video in stories. Tap it and find a library full of hundreds of thousands of moving stickers powered by GIPHY. Using this feature consistently can add a ton of personality to your Instagram stories and help you build a loyal follower. You can get an Instagram tutorial step-by-step on how to add GIFs here to Instagram Stories.

How to Plan and Schedule your Instagram Stories for Business

Daily sharing on Instagram stories is key to building a following and reinforcing your impressions, and you can schedule your stories just like other media articles in your material calendar.

Planning your regular Instagram feed content together with your Instagram stories will help to keep things cohesive and clear.

Building a quick Instagram storyboard and making sure it flows is a great way to get going. You will guarantee that all the important points are discussed by outlining the beginning, middle, and end of your story, while still maintaining that everything flows naturally.

Why it's possible to plan Instagram stories for later:

1. Begin by dragging your stories and lowering them to the storyboard device and then rearranging them to suit the order and look you like. You can also easily resize and crop images to fit Instagram Stories' 9:16 ratio.

2. First, you should add links or translations to your intended stories when it's time to post. This helps you drive traffic and sales by taking the time to write insistent subtitles and CTAs.

3. First, select your Instagram story's time and date for the planning.

Four from the Save Story icon's drop-down list. When it comes to writing, you should be told about your mobile phone. And after you open the message, download the stories to your phone and subtitle or copy links into the clipboard so that Instagram stories can be posted in seconds. Planning Instagram stories is one of the best things you can do on Instagram in 2019 to grow your business! Later on, you will have to upgrade to a paid plan to schedule stories.

5.7 Shout them out

Give them a direct message once you have done your research and established which accounts you can share content with.

Ask them to credit the image you want to go viral to your account. Also, it's not out of the question to ask them to direct them to check your page and follow you.

Propose you do the same with a picture of your choice for them.

If you're starting, providing your photos free of charge is commonplace.

But the exposure has immense value, and an unmeasurable amount increases your chances of a viral post.

5.8 Post behind-the-scene content

You may find a lull in your Instagram content queue between product postings and promotional content. One of the best techniques to fill this gap is with content behind the scenes- often undervalued content. There is an excellent reason to "create" or "how-to" content across all channels-people like to be in the know. "Post contents that display more than just the brand, e.g., highlight your staff or the environment of your business. These types of posts are attractive and can help you establish stronger connections with fans, supporters, and potential clients.

5.9 Share research warning and trends

Helping people move further into new research subjects is another powerful way to drive shares first one's placement, with the label "it's not what you expect" is very successful, despite conventional knowledge challenges.

The second most mentioned was to live longer, long life's secret; now who wouldn't want it! The solution may not be to avoid men, though, when one instance is not scientific evidence! One of the top U.S. posts today showed the opposite view of a long life. So maybe to be married is moral for men who want to live a long time? This way, this article dominated the most shared content for USA Today because it was warm-hearted, joyful, and encouraging.

It is therefore agreed that it will also do well to share new research. The same tale of dependence, along with some other research-based items, is seen in social media.

Warnings are another type of research into more directives. The research that we mentioned earlier suggested sharing people to warn people about things. This seems to be the case if we look at the most shared content on Instagram 2 of its usually shared top 3 posts are cautionary tales.

Trends Keep your users informed by keeping hashtags and jumping in the socially active trends in all communications and keeping you informed about user needs.

CHAPTER 6: GROWING FOLLOWERS

6.1 How to get more Instagram followers

Despite organic reach on a steep decline, attracting more followers on Instagram is more challenging than ever. But not impossible!

There are a few things to grow your Instagram follower count. First of all, you need to create the content of high quality that resonates with the audience. You must also optimize your content to reach as many users as possible. And finally, to encourage new visitors to press the "Follow" button, you need to optimize your Instagram profile.
We will concentrate on the second step in this chapter: tactics to refine your posts to reach a wider audience.

#1: Finding the Right Hashtags for Your Business When used appropriately, Instagram hashtags will help you grow your scope, become more involved, and gain more followers.

But to be successful with hashtags, you need to be strategic about what hashtags you're using and when you're using them. While Instagram's most popular hashtags have been used millions of times, that doesn't mean you're going to get a ton of likes with comments just by adding #love, #happy, or #dog to your posts.

Rather than using the popular Instagram hashtags, it's best to use the Instagram hashtags having an engaging community behind them and relevant to the audience or industry. So how should you find these cool, creative, and community-oriented hashtags?

Well, the best way is to see what Instagram hashtags are already being used by your audience, competitors, and industry leaders. The narrower the hashtag's scope, the more users tend to be engaged. And how niche hashtags can get you would be shocked!

For example, a coffee shop based in Toronto would like to use hashtags such as #specialty coffee (describes their business), #coffeeshopvibes (describes your account's purpose), and #TOcoffee or #coffeeovers (depicts your target market). You can then add specific hashtags, such as #spading, #chinatownTO, or even #Toronto, to your location.

You can also use Instagram hashtags that have an active community around them, so you could use #dailycortado instead of using #coffee, which has fewer posts but a more engaged audience. If you need some help finding a niche and industry-specific hashtags, then you might want to check out the Latter's Hashtag Suggestions feature.

Hashtag Suggestions works by finding relevant hashtags for your posts automatically based on other hashtags you are using.

Let's say we're posting a photo of a lovely bedroom, for example, to promote your business selling linens. All you need to do is no one relevant hashtag (like #live), put it in Hashtag Suggestions, hit "Suggest," and the feature will generate 30 other hashtags, sorted by relevance, immediately.

Then you can choose which hashtag to add to your post. All you need to do is click "Insert Hashtags" and add them to your caption's end.

You can test your Instagram Insights to see how many views come from hashtags if you have an Instagram business account. If the amount is small, try adding a couple of specific labels to see if you can lift it.

#2: Hack the Instagram Stories for More Awareness 2018 has been a big year for Instagram Stories. And as organic reach for regular Instagram posts continues to drop, we expect stories to become even more critical for a business to engage with their followers and remain top of mind.

Yet, did you know that reports from Facebook can also help you gain followers from Twitter?

Instagram stories appearing on the Explore page, meaning you can still find and watch your stories from people who don't even follow them.

And they like what they see; they could even follow you! This is another excellent reason always to try to have an active Instagram story up. But besides appearing on the Explore page, accounts can also look for different locations and hashtags on the Search pages. As we wrote in an earlier chapter, they have their own stories attached to most Instagram geo-locations and hashtags. While this is an underused Instagram feature, we expect it to become more prevalent in the coming year as Instagram users become more comfortable watching and creating stories.

#3: Boosting your Instagram posts to reach new Instagram audiences may not be as popular as Facebook advertising, but such organic reach declining on Instagram, it is not a bad idea to start investing in boosting.

It's not that difficult to run your own Instagram ad campaign, but it can intimidate many small business owners and influencers who haven't experienced it before.
Fortunately, it's easy to boost Instagram posts to get Instagram followers!

You don't need to build complex Instagram advertisements in Facebook business manager, all you have to do is make an Instagram post like you usually do and then press the "promote" button once it's posted. Instagram already draws in a "similar audience" that you can send the post with, or you can easily create your following in the app by selecting an interest, age range, and the sexes you like.

For example, if you post a photo of a thousand-year-old taco shop in Los Angeles, you will promote your post for people who are interested in tacos, live in Los Angeles, and are between 20-35 years of age.

Make sure you set the goal of "profiling visits" and make sure you've got an eye-catching image and a captivating caption.

The only distinction is the "supported" indication at the top and the call-to-action button. Start with a small daily budget and run the ad for 1-2 days to get going. Instagram advertisements are science, so be prepared to change your posts and viewers until you get the results you expect!

6.2 Organic followers a crucial part

Being a digital product also tempts owners to take shortcuts for cheaper, short-lived benefits. For faster results, influencers, brands, and creators have tried to buy followers and expand their reach. Many of them had desired results, but it didn't help to take the business forward.

Buying followers on Instagram will increase the site's number of followers. In no way would this fair amount help to strengthen partnerships, revenue, or visibility.

The customers you target wouldn't like, retweet or comment on your comments to increase the number of followers, they won't buy your services/products. That's why the secret to planning an Instagram growth strategy is raising organic fans.

The number of followers on Instagram often affects how customers view your brands. It is accepted that business accounts with fewer followers are less credible than those with more. We tend to buy followers for this reason.

There's a way out of this loop, however. There are some fun and effective ways on Instagram to create real followers.

Here are some excellent tricks to help you build an effective growth strategy for Instagram.

6.3 Hashtags and their effectiveness

The world is going around, especially on Instagram, with hashtags in the social media landscape. You can choose the right hashtags or break your post. It has a significant effect on the dedication the post gets and can be a substantial determinant if your message hits the hands of the target market or not.

Although there are several different hashtag methods, the perfect mix is still up for discussion. I also discovered, in my own experience, that those that are geographically or categorically related to your article are the most powerful hashtags.

Although it may get a lot of love with hashtags as "# love" or "# friends," they are usually from bots-and this is an insignificant vanity metric that won't get any results for your company. Instead, research and find out what local companies and companies are using in your industry. This ensures that you always reach the right people.

In every industry, countless accounts are trying to gather a community to pay attention to its content.

You will add a link for user-submitted images and a whole universe of followers that you might not enter without them.

The more marks you get, the stronger. Images with more labels tended to be more fun.
Some features make Instagram a powerful tool for people's engagement. For starters, hashtags are a perfect way to follow conversations within your niche and find consumers

who are interested in your product. Check hashtags to see people in your community who already chat about your product online.

It allows you to recognize Instagram influencers in your industry and expand your Instagram afterward.

Hashtags started on Twitter to get the most out of Instagram hashtags and are a staple of Instagram marketing while never taking off on Facebook. Just by inserting text after the #symbol in Instagram, bio, or post, every word or phrase can be turned into a clickable topic.

When users click, all public posts tagged with this hashtag are taken. Maybe even more important, users are now also able to follow hashtags that interest them. This provides them a stream of content that does not support the poster using hashtags. It is an excellent way for users to find content that they are interested in and — for dealers to expand their content reach.

To fully expand the reach and get the most out of Instagram marketing, you need to use the right kind of Instagram hashtags.

The different types of hashtags are available.
The primary forms of hashtags are crucial to the incorporation of e-commerce firms in their marketing strategy.

Location hashtags: Location labeling is also critical because your images appear when people search the area. In addition to the tags, you should also focus on using emoji in your branded hashtags for Instagram: most brands will (and should) have a unique hashtag. You must add this to every article, place it in your profile, and encourage users to apply it to posts in which they share content created by users. It can include your brand name, but not — for example, Fashion Nova's hashtag #Nova Babe.

Contest hashtags: This is a branded hashtag created for a particular contest. These are often used to identify competition entries for photo submission competitions and to generate overall awareness of games. In addition to the main advertised hashtag competition, general campaign hashtags such as #instacontest and #giveaway should also be included.

Hashtags of the general appeal: some hashtags are popular with a wide range of people. This can help you reach your comments greatly because they are more likely to be searched out. Of starters, #nonfilter, #antiques, #ilovemyjob and #puppylove are the examples.

Niche-specific hashtags: Each industry has sentences and keywords that are only relevant to its target audience. These hashtags will not get you as much as the hashtags of the general appeal, but they will provide you with more traffic like #harrypotter (if you offer accessories influenced by the Harry Potter series).

Hashtags: Current events and seasonal holidays may make great hashtags, particularly in sales-oriented vacations such as Valentine's Day or Christmas. People will probably be looking for relevant content right now, so make use of a few #valentineformyvalentine and #stockingstuffer hashtags.

Entertaining hashtags: they won't help you to meet you, but they'll help you entertain and develop your brand. It was meant to be purely funny or smart, and that is it — E.G., #iknowitstooearlyforChristmas,and#thisiswhyweallhatemonda. Often entertaining hashtags may be grouped one by one to tell a story such as #iknowitstooearlyforChristmas #toobad #itshereanyway.

For best results, do work on each of these hashtags and use various hashtag variations for your articles in each section. This will improve marketing and enable you to attract the largest and most important market possible.

Hashtag best practices Hashtag use is one of the most critical determinants of your popularity on Instagram and, unexpectedly, they are a little difficult to crack.

Fortunately, you will benefit from the following best practice to maximize your reach and results:

- List your branded hashtag on your profile.
- Include some amusing hashtags, which are most likely to be read, at the very beginning of your hashtag page.
- Use a lot of hashtags. The cap is thirty hashtags per message. However, numerous case studies have found that between eight and 11 hashtags for each post are a sweet spot, especially if the types of hashtags are diversified.
- Turn the hashtags up.
- Switch up. On every job, don't use the same hashtags. Create hashtag groups that can be cycled for various posts. This not only improves the exposure to different audiences, but it also avoids Instagram's flagging your profile as spamming.
- Take the time to search for every hashtag. Which can help you discover new hashtags to make sure you don't use a forbidden hashtag unintentionally or leap into a subject without knowing what it means.

Uses **product tags** for better marketing practice Instagram now enables product tags and product stickers that can be used for business profiles (with approval) and enables users to tap the product in a post or story, get more information and go to the website to buy.

Shopify allows retailers to integrate this streamlined shopping experience and label items into articles and stories and potential customers without needing to see a connection in their organics.

This choice is not only extremely convenient for users to switch, but also addresses the biggest marketing obstacle for Instagram to add links to post, making it easy for users to tap and buy.

It is easy to set up an Instagram sales channel for your Shopify store to make the deal even sweeter. Here you can see exactly how you can do this.

Traders can also directly integrate an Instagram gallery on their site, creating a complete integration. In this way, users can visit Instagram to view material evidence and enjoy reviews and be encouraged to purchase more by-product tags.

Instagram on-site galleries are quick and straightforward to set up, thanks to shopping apps such as Instafeed and Instagram shopping galleries.

6.4 Linking out to customized pages

Many social platforms require clickable links or hyperlinks on their posts, whether it's a status update, tweet, or video description on the YouTube channel.

Instagram is a bit different from that.
Besides the profile section of your brand, clickable-links are not allowed anywhere else.
The Instagram photo and comment areas are strictly designed to engage and improve user experience. If you're trying to add a reference here, you're going to seem to be spam.

This chooses where to link-out, particularly important. Notice how the link guides visitors to the homepage of your website.

For visitors, clicking on such link breaks contexts, causes confusion and harms conversion. A visitor effectively leaves from consuming images of motorcycle accessories to a static homepage where they may
End up confused and leave the page.

So, concluding, where should clickable-link point to?
Here are a few ideas:

Option 1: Instagram-content landing page. Fortunately, links will lead visitors to dedicated landing pages. On this page, you should provide additional photo or content-related information and context on your Profile. Especially in e-commerce or running a digital store.

It is increasing pressure and lets aspiring shoppers buy items quickly. They don't have to waste time searching your site to find what they just saw on Instagram. For example, Made well's Instagram pages feature high-quality product images. The URL even suggests click-through will lead to a customized Instagram-related landing page. Items on their landing page are recognizable instantly. For potential customers with added quick-links for streamline checkout, the same items are provided.

Option 2: Long-form content. Unfortunately, Instagram purchases are rare. Target audiences in most industries (especially B2B) require lead nurturing before conversion.
In such cases, your clickable link should lead visitors to long-form content like a blog, newsletters, or videos that further educate and groom potential among clients.
 As a popular social media management tool, Hootsuite leads traffic to a pre-recorded social media strategy webinar. In this webinar, Hootsuite focuses on quality rather than selling the business. Focusing on social media Trends in the webinar

lead to an opt-in e-book resource. By funneling profit, Hootsuite entices readers to become a subscriber.

6.5 How to Track Your Impressions, Reach, Engagement, and More

Now let's look at the content metrics of Instagram and what each means. Within Instagram Insights, you will be able to find tons of information about your performance of content under the heading "Content."

By type of content (photos, images, carousel articles, and shopping posts), as well as days, months, and years, you can filter this information.

Impressions
 Are the total number of visualizations of your post. This number includes users scrolling through their feed, clicking a photo view through the profile of your business, or viewing the content directly through an Instagram Direct Message.
Range Like perceptions, the range also corresponds to your content's overall number of views, but this time it's the number of unique pictures (unique users who watched the content).

Engagements

This is the cumulative number of times you supported, saved, or commented on your message. Please remember that Instagram will not record multiple comments from the same person, which may arise in the case of gifts where people appear to post multiple times to improve their chances.

Engagement Level

Although Instagram Insights does not include the engagement level information, Instagram advertising is still a critical metric.

The level of participation is the number of fans or viewers interested in your comments. Generally speaking, if you want to calculate your Instagram average engagement rate, your follower count will divide the number of likes and comments, giving you a percentage.

You can take the total number of comments you received on a per-post basis, say 1200, and divide it by your followers, like 15,000, and then multiply it by 100 to get your percentage. In this scenario, the level of contribution to this article would be 8%.

Instagram Insights

Profile Visits & Followers will also tell you how many times your profile has been viewed and how many accounts you have started after.

Sadly, Instagram does not include information about your development in fans, which is how many followers you have gained or lost over some time. That being said, manually calculating this number is not too hard. You can also use an Instagram advertising app from a third party to do this for you.

When you're searching for a reliable and robust Instagram analytics platform from third-party apps, you might want to check out the new Instagram Analytics from Later.

When you track the analytics of your account with Later, when you schedule Instagram posts and plan your feed, you can quickly review your insights and apply your lessons to your strategy.

For example, if you see more feedback on Instagram posts with people in them, you can take the intuition and adapt your content strategy automatically by planning more people-focused updates.

One of the easiest ways to identify which forms of content that connect with your audience is to watch the Instagram engagement rate. And you can easily integrate more of that material into your approach until you recognize what works best for your audience.

Instagram Analytics

Later also tracks Instagram Stories metrics for up to 3 months, so you can easily find insights related to stories and optimize them to get more views, access, answers, and more!

For example, you can figure out which times of the day your Instagram stories get the most outlook and then plan your future stories at those times. Or you can check your metrics and determine the optimal number of accounts you are expected to publish every day or week.

6.6 Some other tips for growing followers

Get Your Supporters Involved by Creating a Facebook Debate, the cornerstone of your social success is your supporters. You do not exist online without them. The key to becoming viral is communicating with your followers within a post.

To do this, you can use a couple of specific viral tactics. Enlist your fans, for instance, to build and share content on a particular topic. I like to ask a question I think deeply about and ask my fans whether they agree or disagree.

It's like setting up a conversation with friends and having the viral capacity for these kinds of comments. Your followers will be more motivated to share their content through your post, thereby increasing the potential for viruses. Involve and inspire the viewers, and you're going to be shocked by how much more exposure the content receives.

Promote your Instagram account through the cross.

Suggest cross-promoting the page through other platforms to marketers involved in through their followers Instagram. If your marketing team innovatively utilizes Instagram, speak about it through a business portal or client blog can make sense.

This can help drive your Instagram channel awareness while positioning your business as a leader in social media marketing.

Based on quality rather than quantity of followers.

Most Instagram advertisers believe it is essential to create a fully customized Instagram profile by having a large number of followers. The more fans a product gets, after all, the more reliable it shows regularly. But a quick look at Instagram accounts operated by some of the world's largest corporations reveals that more important than quantity is the value of the fans. Instagram reports with hundreds of thousands, if not millions, of fans are endless "clickbait."

Those accounts have far more fans than, perhaps, the 42,000 that can assert from Salesforce, a business with a market cap of $74 billion. And yet, given their smaller count of subscribers, no one would assume that Salesforce is a lightweight business with their right minds.

Social media advertisers can focus on developing a strategy that involves target audiences instead of raising followers' numbers to create an aura of legitimacy.
To gain credibility, earn a blue checkmark.

Similar to Facebook, Instagram offers the ability to earn verified account status through a blue checkmark for established brands. A checkmark will provide peace of mind to Instagram followers as they are confident that your profile is your organization's official voice.

While Instagram does not provide a way for the general public to submit a request for verification, Mashable has reported that there are ways to verify an Instagram account by more creative means.

For fun, add emoji.

Instagram is about having fun using different media outlets. One way to use emoji's in your bio company through your Instagram profile. Most emoji will substitute letters, allowing you a few characters to compose a convincing profile. It also serves to show that your company can appeal to younger users, many of whom are on Instagram.

Developing an Instagram profile that is fully optimized and capable of engaging Instagram users will require an organized plan of attack and patience. You will be well ahead of the competition by being able to measure output and being willing to make changes in response to the results.

Yet have they motivated you to gain followers? Human pictures are viewed 60,000 times faster than text. If you want to express a sensation or sentiment easily, emoji are the way to go.

If you want to pay more attention to your message, add a few emoji. The symbol of the core appears to get the most dedication. First of all, it is best to have a good understanding of what each emoji means.

Hub Spot's Emoji Guide is the perfect place to start learning if you begin with emoticons.
After all, you don't want to use an emoji that transmits the wrong message.

Engage the Followers with Plenty of Visual Content

Also, read an article on one year's top viral posts? You may notice that the majority of viral items are visual. It was part of people's digital cycle of focus decreased.

Talk of audio, photos, and GIFs to go viral on social media. Such graphical image types are a standard of social media and can quickly go viral unless done correctly. I love shooting clips of my feelings or interactions. I'm going to whip out my mobile and hit record when the mood strikes me.

You certainly don't have to customize the videos and have a script. Only start recording and speaking from the head. This leads to so much more engagement, as you may not be the only person to feel some way.

CHAPTER 7: ADVERTISEMENT

7.1 Learning follower preferences (usage of analytics)

Instagram has its native analytics tools to provide you with plenty of data on the quality of your site. Note that Instagram analytics are only available for business.
Go to your profile and then click on the graph symbol in the top-right corner to access your analytics.

- Total number of visits to your profiles
- Total number of clicks on web pages
- Total reach (number of unique accounts you have seen posts)
- Full impacts (number of times your posted posts have been viewed)
- The performance of each post including engagement and impressions
- Number of views on your post
- Total views we can see how our expectations, scope, and dedication increase or decrease from month to month and how it affects an increasing or diminishing count of followers.

By contrasting this data with top positions and evaluating their results, you will identify trends and patterns that will help to make the advertising long-term more successful.

You can also gather insights into your published content to see what your audience likes.

Figure out what kind of material attracts the most so that you can see what resonates with the viewer. To improve the Instagram marketing strategy, use this knowledge and create more engaging content.

Sprout's methods for measuring social success is excellent for collecting such observations. In the following example, the message labeling method was used for communities in various campaigns and hashtags, providing a more concise analysis of what messages are more commonly shown as the adage states, "What is calculated is finished." There is a range of Instagram tools available that provide informative Instagram analytics to make brands on the channel more successful.

When searching for an Instagram analytics tool, most marketing teams need several capabilities. First of all, the device should be able to monitor post-performance to display which posts are most active, best engaged, and best rate clicked. Marketers can use Instagram more efficiently from there.

Marketers will also like to use a tool that can schedule posts in advance. Some Instagram analytical tools will decide when is the best time to share content to make a post-work. This time may be outside office time, which can be useful for scheduling content.

Eventually, many advertisers will want to use a platform for Instagram analytics, which can track talk for unique keywords and hashtags. This enables marketing teams to connect to customers or prospects in real-time to create memorable experiences.

To customize your profile and plan for Instagram.

The only way to know what the Instagram plan succeeds is by testing it. While an Instagram business account offers simple quality data, third-party monitoring services provide a variety of otherwise unavailable details.

A third-party analytics system is essential from the measurement of the reference in your Instagram bio to the determination of which postings echo the most with followers to determine the perfect time to post new content.

7.2 Build a following of highly engaged fans

Instagram ads all have the same targeting options as Facebook ads. These include location-based targeting, demographics, preferences, behavior, audiences looking at, and automatic targeting (let Facebook decide).

Perhaps better, you can reach custom audiences on Instagram. Custom customers are groups of people who have, in some way, already linked to your product. You might be able to visit your website, engage with Facebook posts, use your app, or share your contact information with you.

Target niche groups and communities a primary consumer discovery mode of day one. In June, the network expanded the exploration of hashtags with a new Explore page to make discovery "immediate and straightforward."

Identify and use common hashtags to make your target audience more accessible. Finding the right tags may take some work, but the most important and commonly used findings are obtained. Here are a couple of ways: locate and search for rivals and peer organizations.

Using Instagram search–plug-in and go from main terms and phrases. Often a hashtag takes you to the next one.

Identify the target's active users. Do you use tags that are relevant to you and about what you are?

There are many niche groups within the global Instagram community that use hashtags to communicate. If you can find them, they are gold. For example, there's an active #igersmaine photo group here in Maine. This Hashtag would be a perfect way to gain exposure in a spot or place of scenic appeal; #dogsofinstagram could be a more famous example of a niche hashtag. For a dealer who sells dog toys and accessories, this would be a good fit.

It's not enough for you to find your Instagram target audience if you don't know what to do with the information.

Once you have an understanding of the target audience is, and what they want, you can use the knowledge to target Instagram successfully. Here are some tips to help reach your audience on Instagram: identifying and studying your target audience. Let's start with a few principal approaches to set up your target audience on Instagram. You'll also find some tips on research for the audience so you can learn how to target an Instagram audience.

1. Start with more famous people. The wheel does not need to be worked back. If your organization has already identified buyer people, reusing the same data will often make sense to identify the target audience.

Give your business a clear idea of what the typical customer looks like. Ask yourself what your goods are and what they are doing. Who's ready for your product? And what does your audience seek?

For example, a tool like Evernote encourages the taking of notes and organizing of valuable information for people.

As a matter of general terms, their target group would be

- busy professionals
- Looking for solutions to coordinate their data and activities
- And to increase productivity.

2. You can learn a lot about the audience by looking at the Instagram audience of your competitors. See what kind of followers you have and what types of posts you write. This can give you a sense of how your target audience on Instagram will look. You will see if you have holes or incomplete audience segments when you have begun to take a picture of your crowd.

While the Phalanx Influencer Auditor is designed for influencer research, it is also an excellent instrument for the analysis of your competitors. Only enter your social media handle, and the software produces a detailed account audit report.

You will discover essential insights for the audience, such as their places, population, and brand names.

3. Use existing demographic data. You can learn a lot about your Instagram target audience from your Instagram analytics.

Go to "Audience" under "Insights." Here you can view some vital statistics on the ages, gender, and location of your existing followers.

Combine this information with your buyer and the information you have gathered from competitor research. This should help you paint a clear picture of how your target audience in Instagram looks.

4. Conduct social listening to understand the relevant talks. Public research is one of the main steps to understand and effectively target your audience and Instagram.

Social listening is one of the ways to understand the Instagram target audience. You will have difficulty understanding how to engage your audience unless you know what your audience is talking about and what they are interested in.

You are using Sprout Social listening software to identify discussions in your company and on specific topics. It gives a better sense of what your target audience is thinking about how they feel about a particular subject and who leads such discussions.

It helps you to recognize trendy talks and prominent personalities to help you reinforce your product message.

5. Take advantage of Instagram polls. Why not ask them directly if you are going to research your audience?

Take advantage of the Instagram Stories surveys to ask specific questions to help you understand your audience better and improve your Instagram content.

You might ask them what content they want and what they expect from you. Or you can build surveys to filter your likings and dislikes, your passions and loves, your shopping behavior, etc.

Execute several highly-targeted accounts. It is inefficient to target all your customers on a single Instagram account.

Some brands have several customers to please. Trying such a monumental task from one account increases the risk that some groups become separated and adds uncertainty to your website.

This is how you can solve here:

Creating multiple Instagram accounts to divide customer acquisition into highly focused networks where you can better address that person's fears, concerns, and pain points.

Here are some suggestions about the material to host supplementary accounts:

Highlight various uses of your product. If your company provides more than one product, each product may have a different purpose.

Brands, for example, tend to have several items with specific reasons, such as anti-aging, make-up, and hair care, in the cosmetics industry.

Two should address each singular purpose. Geographical distribution your consumers will find themselves in different fields with different interests, perspectives, and lifestyles unless your product is strongly local.

To counter these regional and international differences, create separate Instagram accounts.

Whole Foods makes excellent use of this innovation with numerous national product accounts across the US.

Here's their Miami account page. Note how the Miami account sounds summery, while Chicago feed concentrates more on winter-related soups and ales.
Furthermore, such segregation makes it possible for Whole Foods to promote local organic products that conform to its brand character.

Option 1: Offer special reductions. Some things happen when rewarding Instagram followers with exclusive discount; First, increase your brand's exposure as followers are using word-of-mouth to disseminate your brand name to their families and friends, which entices them to join you.

Most importantly, you build a relationship that ensures that supporters return.

Option 2: Give Sneak peeks another chance to make your fans feel unique show an item to your customers before it hits the market. It creates excitement, hype, and demand for your brand.

When the product is released, people will eagerly buy it, creating a further hype.
Alternatively, you can look into everyday life in your company behind the scenes.
It humanizes the brand and makes an emotional connection possible for followers. It also creates loyalty as followers feel they belong to a genuine and trustworthy family.
Form stack wants its followers to realize that they are not just a dark tool to construct form. They are real people with interests close to you

7.3 Instagram advertisement door to marketing

Instagram ads aren't quite a secret, but they're not used almost enough by brands. We always recommend ads on social media, especially on Instagram and Facebook, if we conduct campaigns for our clients here at Wish pond. Due to the active targeting of the platform, you can advertise directly for the people you know are most interested in your product. In addition to the apparent gain of reaching new potential customers, marketing allows you to incorporate CTAs, ensuring that ad audiences can be sent to the landing pages on your web for purchasing. Sometimes you need to compensate for games-but advertisements always push the buck up in the boom.

In the past, you used sponsored posts because you chose to advertise on Instagram. This includes secretly engaging with influencers from Instagram and convincing them to promote their brand. Although this can be a very efficient way of driving traffic and purchases through Instagram ads, it is restricted:

Sometimes expensive.
It requires access and negotiation.
If they do not produce zero transparency or solution.
A specific sampling of the market.

In Instagram ads, sponsored posts still have their location. Having someone else to sell the brand has excellent advantages. It offers material evidence, adds a cool factor to your business, and people can buy something if they first trust. Moreover, even though you don't have much control over the influencers, you have no choice about who to target.

Sponsored posts are still an excellent way to influence the market, mainly if you sell a product. And they're not the only way influencers can be leveraged. In October 2017, Instagram launched paid partnerships to enhance user transparency and provide more Instagram opportunities for brands and influencers alike. Its functionality, open for Instagram-adherent profiles and obligations, offers greater transparency and monitoring than regular sponsored posts. After 2015, everybody can also learn how to create Instagram advertisements via the self-supporting Facebook advertising platform. With it, you have total control over and who sees your ads. Your ads are posted directly from your account, as opposed to sponsored postings and paid partnerships. The advantages of this Instagram marketing approach include:

Scalable pricing.
Through self-service.
Robust coverage to command you.
Highly refined targeting of the audience.

Furthermore, when switching Instagram from a linear timeline to a curate list, you never know how many of your fans will see your content.

Instagram ads appear on the site, like any other regular post. There are a few ad choices, but mostly they're pretty similar. And they are much less complicated than other network advertising such as Twitter.
Nevertheless, reaching the market is much better.

For example, if you want your post to be larger or smaller, you can add pictures of different sizes.

Since Instagram is geared for mobile users, you will consider the screen size while making advertisements.

Ads on Instagram may not be the safest place to sell. And as the overall goal is to get viral, it is better to concentrate here on the "top of the funnel."

Concentrate instead on branding, views, clicks, and more. Once users find you and start your Instagram journey, the rest follows. Besides the regular old photo ad, Instagram also offers carousel ads above. This is great for consumer presentations that require multiple images to tell the entire story.

Instagram has two other types of ads: Video,
Stories.

If you are an expert on Facebook ads, just using interest-based targeting while performing Instagram advertising. And, to promote clients and re-engage guests, full of email users, former customers, and more. But you can never say which ad is the strongest to accomplish or viral your goals. You're going to want to run a few experiments to get a ton of money spent on Instagram advertising. Compare how certain ads perform with socialinsight.io engagement tracking.

With this feature, you will see how many people on any given day engage with your posts. InstaStories are powerful if they use them right so that we will deal with them.

How to create ads for Instagram?
Link your profile with Instagram to Facebook page
Create a campaign for Instagram
Create a set of 4 advertisements.
Analyze your Instagram ads and optimize them. Let's learn how you can create your first Instagram ad.
Step1: Connect your Instagram account to your Facebook page. Linking your Instagram account to your Facebook page is the first step in creating an Instagram ad. Only once do you need this?
Visit your Facebook page Settings and click "Instagram Ads." then, click "Log in" and fill in your credentials for Instagram login. You can also build one now if you don't already have an Instagram account.

Step 2: Creating an Instagram ad campaign after linking your Instagram account to your Facebook page, it's time to go to the Advertising Manager and create your first campaign. Users can also create Instagram ads there if they are more

comfortable using the Power Editor. If you are already creating Facebook ads, you will be familiar with much of this process.
Tap on the "Campaigns" tab in the Advertising Manager and then"+ Build" near the screen's top-left corner.

Step 3: Build your Instagram ad set On the Ad Set tab, you will be able to select "Buy" as the conversion form you want to customize

Next, define who you would like to see your ads and how much money you would like to spend. With Instagram advertising, there are all the same targeting options available for Facebook ads. If you have already built some custom audiences, you can pick them at this point to target with your Instagram ad.

Next, choose the Placements ad on Instagram, as well as Facebook and Messenger, you'll see the option to run your campaign.

Start low when you figure out how much you want to spend on Instagram advertising. If your ad performs well, you can always increase the budget later. When you have done choosing who to aim and how much to pay, in the bottom right, press "Continue."

You will see an option to select your Instagram ad format on the next page. Note that Instagram does not support the

Canvas format. Scroll down to upload images or videos once you have decided.

Scroll down further after you have downloaded your graphics, and you will see a choice on the left to add text to an ad.

Finally, you will be able to preview how your ad will look on Instagram to the right of the text editor. Here's how it seems like an example commercial. You can also see the look of your ad in any other chosen format.

Check ideas to find the most successful, innovative, and targeted messaging. You can edit your Instagram ad within Ads Manager to incorporate split testing, change targeting parameters, and view analytics for your ad performance.

Instagram's first ad is always the toughest. Once you've won the beginning, the second time around, it's going to be much more comfortable.

Types of Instagram advertising

You can run Instagram ads in five different types:

Photo Ads a Photo Ad is a candid photo in landscape or square format. In terms of visual asset needs, these are the simplest, as you only need a single image. Here is an example of a Fimbulvetr Snowshoes outdoor e-commerce brand Photo Ad that takes users to the snowshoe product page featured in the ad creative.

Live Advertising Instagram used to have a live limit of 15 seconds, but this restriction has since been removed. Now, videos in landscape or square format can be up to 60 seconds long and shot. Through its Instagram advertising, Dollar Shave Club uses the Video Ad format for advertising a new membership deal, showcasing the various items included through the agreement.

Instagram Carousel Ads can have two to ten images, and videos from anywhere users can see through. West Elm uses Carousel Advertising to demonstrate its product range for its Instagram advertising campaigns.

Slideshow ads are just like video ads as they appear as a clip in user feeds. Such advertisements consist, however, of a series of still images, similar to a slideshow, that serves as a clip. On the slideshow, you can add audio and text to your ads.

Stories Advertising Instagram Stories Ads is one of the most popular types of ads for businesses on the site. Instagram stories are similar to Snapchat, which allows users and marketers to share self-destructing photos and videos. Brands can also advertise photo or video content in Instagram Stories. Instagram Stories Ads actively used online clothing retailer ASOS in establishing brand recognition and recall ads.

Instagram ad campaign targets Brand awareness Brand Reach Traffic app installs Engagement Video views Lead generation conversions You can select from several campaign objectives when you advertise on Instagram. These are potential targets for your Instagram ad campaign that you pick from a list. Do not forget that: the way your Instagram advertisements are structured and how you pay for them will be affected.

For instance, you probably don't care about how many users click on your link if you want people to see your video.

You can already know the campaign goals of creating Facebook ads. Options are: This brand awareness is aimed at promoting your company, product, app, or service knowledge in Instagram ads. This objective, formerly known as consciousness, falls within this objective. The Brand awareness objective assists in photo advertising, photo ads, carousel ads, slideshow ads, and stories ads.

You can also raise awareness of the business, product, app, or service with an objective. The objectives are formerly known as local awareness, and reach & frequency are now part of this goal. The Reach target supports all forms of Instagram advertising. Brand Awareness is different from Brand Awareness because it allows you to reach a wider audience, while Brand Awareness targets people more likely to recall your ad or brand.

You can use traffic to drive visitors to your website. If you've got a mobile app, this also works for driving apps. The target previously called Clicks Website is now transported. This goal can also be used to create an offer for your audience. The traffic goal supports all forms of Instagram advertising.

The App Installs target is appropriate if you are trying to get users to download your app. With the App Installs objective, you can use any form of Instagram ad Here is a Carousel Ad example from Postmark, which allows users to download the mobile app directly to their respective software stores: dedication is another aim that you can use to promote offers. You can also boost your Instagram account and comments. Photo promotions, ads for videos, and ads for slideshows are your choices for interaction.

If you run a Video Ad, Carousel Ad, Slideshow Ad, or Stock Ad, you can use the Video Views goal to promote the video. This is the ultimate goal of becoming aware of your brand and product lines.

Instagram lead generation ads with a Lead Generation target are perfect for collecting user data, including email addresses, so that you can market it in the future. This target funds Instagram advertisements of all types.

The conversions goal is an excellent choice for e-commerce companies who want to drive sales. The purposes are previously known as website transformations, and dynamic ads fall under the target of the current conversion. If you want to improve your Facebook SDK for people who are completing a specific action in your app, you should use translations as your objective.

7.4 Targeting options for advertisement

Having a better sense of who is and will improve your communication plan for your Instagram target audience.

Use the above tips to find, investigate, and engage your audience on Instagram.
Instagram has rapidly entered the world of social media. To more than 300 million people posting more than 70 million images and videos each day, Instagram has evolved from a network of near friends exchanging photographs to a massive product and company ecosystem that shares memories and stories.

Instagram has gradually added advertising to the mix, just like its famous peer networks. Much to the dismay of early adopters, ad-free feed days are gone. But that's not to say that you have to jump on the paid social car to make Instagram the most of your business.

One thing was the same. Instagram is a gem for visual discovery. As an early adopter, for this very cause, I appreciate the program. And I can name a few places, blogs, and products I first discovered here–and now I follow or own them faithfully.

It is not shocking that Forrester considers the product contribution to Instagram to be most active, hitting 4.21%. To put that number into context, Facebook and Twitter hit 0.07% and 0.03%, respectively.

Here are three ways to find your Instagram target audience– completely free of charge.

7.5 Focusing on content before investing in advertisement

As an industry, digital marketing is moving quickly–really quickly. Tools, software, and innovations, which were important just a few years ago, have now become outdated. Marketers in each field and the vertical industry are continually seeking new ways of reaching their audience. Sadly, this revolutionary rate also ensures that digital marketing provides more than its fair share of jargon.

- Content advertising involves the creation of content to promote and promote content through paid channels expressly
- Content advertising isn't identical to content marketing; content advertising doesn't rely on organic, social discoverability or shareholder activity, or SEO
- Native advertisement isn't necessarily the same as content advertising
- Content advertising

7.6 Discounts and promotions

But it's real. Use Instagram as a medium to post offers and deals easily is an undervalued method of advertising. Brands focus too much on building their Instagram aesthetic that they forget. It doesn't mean much if it doesn't drive their business revenue.

Sharing occasional offers (in a post or your story) is an easy way to get fans to behave more aggressively and become clients. It's easy for people on Instagram to admire your products from afar. But once they've been following you for a while, they may completely lose interest. Keeping them engaged with promotions will help you avoid that indifference.

CHAPTER 8: VIDEO TELECASTS A SOURCE OF MARKETING

8.1 HOW to Use Instagram Live for Business

We advise that you get to know the function early if you haven't already. While only 22 percent of businesses went "live" on Instagram in 2017, 55 percent planned to use the feature in 2018, according to a recent survey.

For most companies, the idea of going "online" on Instagram is, unsurprisingly, very overwhelming. Although Instagram Stories gives you the option of pre-recorded video publishing, Instagram Live does not have "retakes."

The fact is, however, that Instagram Live has enormous business value. The app can be an excellent tool to drive new fans and interaction as well as the broader business goals when used appropriately.

Live's two new business-focused features: Share Your Broadcast on Instagram Stories, Instagram Live videos can now be shared post-broadcast on Instagram stories.

Once Instagram Live video is finished, at the bottom of the screen, you will see a "Share" button. It's as easy as that! The live broadcast, whether you decide to add it to the videos, will then remain on your Instagram stories for 24 hours.

Instagram Live is a relaxed place, like Instagram Stories, and you can be as creative as you like! But having a solid game plan is a good idea with all that room for creativity.

1. A recent Instagram Live trend is for companies to use the site for advertising and launching new items. And why isn't that? Building a lot of buzz on the goods is the perfect place to go. Instagram Live is a great place to bring up the excitement of your business, whether you are unveiling a new product line or teasing a future launch.

Take your hottest product and deliberately share tiny details about it to enable this strategy to be used on your live broadcast. The mystery is going to be a frenzy to your followers! Asking viewers to sign up for more information about the teaser on your website.

This strategy adds an element of exclusivity to your live video that can inspire people to act quickly and increase the number of leads you receive.

2. Host Q&As, seminars, and address list tutorials. There are different formats to be followed in your live broadcast, including Q&As, workshops, and tutorials. Each of these models is worth the effort and is expected to give you a lot of

viewers. But, if you want to use Instagram Live to make the most of your business, use it to collect e-mails.

One of the ways is to allow people to ask questions in advance. To do so, you can send an e-mail to the landing page (Share the landing page URL in front of your broadcast) to your followers, or provide an e-mail address for viewers to ask.

3. Promote your marketing & promotions. While Snapchat videos are deemed "ephemeral," nothing is more fleeting than live video on Instagram. Take advantage of this by creating a sense of urgency to watch the show!

One of the easiest ways to boost the ratings is by selling limited-time-only deals that you will only be delivered during the show. If you have a gift, discount, promotion, or another campaign you would like to offer to a select few, announce it in advance! And when you go "live," share with your viewers the coupon or discount code.

Instagram Live has recently added another feature to Instagram Live that allows users to add guests to their live streams.

The feature works by allowing people to stream a video to add anyone watching the video at that time by clicking on the "Add" button at the screen corner. If a user is introduced, he or she will enter you on the monitor in a separate window below yours.

Not only can co-hosting an Instagram Live improve the broadcast participation by accessing a full pool of users. It also opens the door for advertising strategies on Instagram, where two companies or influencer collaborators promote a product.

This may no longer be so elusive, but Instagram Live is still a powerful marketing tool to bring to your arsenal. Brands around the globe are still working tirelessly to evaluate strategies that work better as a forum for Live-and believe me, there are many of them.

You can use Live in many different ways, based on your business goals. If you want to strengthen the connection of your brand with fans, a Q&A is a high starting point. However, life can be used for a ton of other purposes, such as teaching fans how to do something or just keeping them up-to-date with the latest brand news.

If you're hoping to achieve some of the broader Instagram advertising targets, such as driving sales or growing sign-ups, putting a strategy in place is necessary.

8.2 Using IGTV for Business

Although IGTV is only a few months old, it is already making waves in the world of social media. Launched as the first standalone video platform for Instagram, IGTV provides businesses with a new channel to grow, showcase their products, and showcase their creativity. The great thing about IGTV is that it's not necessary to polish your videos super! You might think of it as a step up from your Instagram stories, but it doesn't have to be as perfect or curate as a post or video from Instagram.

How to Get Started with IGTV Videos?

You need to create an IGTV channel before you can upload a video to IGTV. The good news is that IGTV is made simple and easy to use on Instagram!

Signing into the IGTV software is the first move.

Next, in the top right corner, tap the gear icon and select Create Channel.

You will post your first clip to IGTV after your channel is online. Begin by opening the channel by clicking on the main page of your avatar.

To add a new clip to IGTV, press the "+" button to the right of your screen.

Now you can select from your camera roll a vertical or horizontal video.

As far as specifications are concerned, Instagram advises that vertical IGTV clips should have a peak ratio of 9:16 and a minimum ratio of 4:5, whereas horizontal videos should have a total aspect ratio of 16:9 and at least 5:4.

If the video shows up, it might be that it has an incorrect aspect ratio!

Write and add a description to your title. Just like on YouTube, to make it easier for people to find your videos on IGTV, you'll want to add to your description of any relevant keywords.

You can add links as well! That's correct; you can click on the links in your definition and carry them outside the Instagram or IGTV device.

Finally, add a picture of the cover! You can upload your custom cover or select from your video a thumbnail. The cover photo shows up on your channel site and in the sections of IGTV, so make it memorable!

Instagram suggests a 1:1.55 aspect ratio (or 654px 420px) for your cover photo.

And this is it! Now you can upload your Instagram vertical video to IGTV!

You can also share your IGTV video with your Instagram stories by tapping the aircraft icon at the bottom of the video and then select "Add video to your story." Viewers can now watch your IGTV video as a story preview.

Keep an eye on your IGTV Analytics

Because IGTV is such a new format on Instagram, it is difficult to say precisely how different audiences will react to your videos — particularly if you share great content!

That's why keeping an eye on your IGTV analytics, which can be directly accessed from your video, is so important.

You can also see audience retention rate beyond Views, Likes, and Comments, which is how many people watched the video to the end.

You can even see a drop-off graph that shows you where people go from your video.

When determining what improvements (if any) to bring to your IGTV approach, measures like these are crucial. For example, if viewers drop off at the 20-minute mark, you can take that as a sign that the best strategy might not be to create videos that are longer than 20 minutes.

8.3 Tips for Making Great Instagram business Video Posts

Let's take a minute and explore how you can refine your video content to get more traction.

In an environment where interest is becoming increasingly scarce, it can be quite challenging to get your followers to interact with your videos (especially longer ones). Yet having a stunning cover photo is one way to improve your odds. Just as you spend time choosing pictures that look amazing in your update, you need to spend a lot of time selecting a high cover image for your clip. Else, all the hard work you put into creating your clip is going to go to waste!

Try to find one that reflects your video's overall message while choosing a cover photo and has the most substantial chance to stop audiences from scrolling past your content.

Don't rely on Instagram sound videos in the feed, but they don't automatically start playing sound. Viewers have to tap on the video to hear the music.

Since you're trying to capture product attention in the first couple of seconds, it's essential to keep in mind that even without sound, your videos need to be clearly understood!

Therefore, your videos should be as beautiful as the photographs used to see your followers on your feed. Even if the audience doesn't have the overall effect, you want them to see the Instagram video plot— also if it's quiet.

Focus on Your Video's First Few Seconds With so much to see on Instagram, creating video content that captures the attention of people within the first 3-5 seconds is essential.

By focusing on your video's first few seconds and making them amazing, you're bound to get better rates of completion and engagement on video.

Find a video length that works for the audience. Just because the duration of your Instagram videos can be 60 seconds doesn't mean it should be. Like all social media things, keeping your audience engaged over a more extended period is difficult.

To find one that works best for the audience, try experimenting with different video lengths. Focus on creating shorter video content if you notice better metrics on your videos that are below 30 seconds. If your videos are longer than your shorter ones, stick to them.

Use a third-party app to edit the Instagram video. There are plenty of tools and applications you can use to not only improve the quality of your images but also apply to advertise to them, whether it's your icon, font, or some other graphic feature.

How to Use Instagram Videos for Business?

What you can do with Instagram video snippets is no end, and it's so easy to have them on your page!

However, it's a good idea to consider a specific goal of communicating your brand image, highlighting your goods, or incorporating your company culture. Here are a few examples of recent video posts: Promote the Goods because, in a short time, videos can relay a ton of information, they are an incredible resource for businesses selling products or services.

Only think about how much more you will be able to display in a 60-second clip than just one picture of your items!

More to that point, according to Hub spot, 64 percent of people are more likely to purchase a product online after first watching a video of it. And seeing your Instagram video in motion could be a great way to increase your Instagram advertising ROI!

Creating videos that express your brand message or share your business culture in Instagram Brand Trust Sharing is a great way to boost trust with your fans and customer

@foodora an excellent example of this. The meal delivery company also posts lovely video content related to their target market and offers them interest to inform your audience. Do you have a subject on which you would like to educate your audience? Maybe it's a tasty dish or a make-up tutorial? Whatever the concentration, sharing fast, snackable content via Instagram video posts is a great strategy.

The idea is that if you have a fascinating subject, you know you'd enjoy learning about it, it's a great strategy to use Instagram videos to do it.

Ready to start preparing Instagram videos? Later, you can schedule video posts from Instagram, optimize the analytics success of your videos, and more!

CHAPTER 9: BECOMING AN INFLUENCER

9.1 Leverage social media influencers naturally

Another essential way to increase your social media viral chances is to use the support and follow-up in influencers of social media. Using influencers expands your social reach, increases engagement, and increases your count of followers.

Even if you are a media influencer yourself, this viral tactic is useful. Now I don't also rely on the standard way on influencers like seeking specific individuals to support my company, songs, or services. Then, I let advertising control occur naturally.

For starters, I'm only going to post pictures of inspiring people I'm fortunate to interact with, and they're going to follow automatically like this one from Eric Schurenberg Inc. and me.

If you don't find inspiring people, how do you learn to use online influencers? Place yourself in your followers ' boots. Who else follows your followers besides you? Who are they reading and resonating with? These are the influencers with whom you should work to make your social posts go viral.

Connect and set up a cross-promotional event with these influencers. You can even combine this with a marketing network created by the client, with influencers sharing their content with their followers.

The following viral tips and tricks are just the beginning, and you can leverage other tactics on each social post once you master a few. I still keep in touch and communicate with my fans, since interacting with them in a meaningful manner is essential to the growth of viral and social value. In my social playbook, this is always what's in yours?

9.2 How to Find the Right Influencers for Your Business?

It can be a considerable challenge to find the best influencers for your Instagram marketing campaign, but it helps to set clear targets. For instance, if your goal is to rack up a lot of engagement, it may make sense to partner with smaller audiences but higher engagement rates with micro-influencers. If you're trying to raise awareness of your product, measures like scope and volume will be more useful.

Don't you know where to start? In determining whether to collaborate with an Instagram influencer, there are four things to keep in mind:

1. Check their Instagram commitment. When an influencer has a high rate of engagement, it means that their followers pay attention to their content and take action. This is why most

companies and social media agencies use engagement to assess who is an ideal influencer.

Generally speaking, you want to see a 2-3 percent contribution rate on the comments of influencers. A 4-6 percent ratio is excellent, while posts are considered "viral" in the tens and twenties.

2. You should align your business with influencers that have "pull" with your target audience. For instance, if you're a fitness brand, it makes sense to partner with influencers like yoga instructors or powerlifters who share a similar audience with your ideal customers.

Aligning your company with an influencer who has "power" with target customers is one of the best techniques to get in front of the right eyes, increase awareness of your name, and display your goods creatively.

3. As mentioned above, the number of followers an influencer has is not as relevant as it used to be — especially now that the Instagram algorithm seems to affect the interaction of larger accounts.

As we have observed, the level of interaction continues to decrease as the number of followers grows. Influencers with fewer followers often maintain higher rates of engagement on their posts, while influencers with large audiences tend to see lower rates of participation and less direct communication with their followers.

That being said, partnering with influencers with important follow-ups is not a bad idea! Just make sure your business is a good fit.

4. Budget Requirements another thing to bear in mind is how much they charge when deciding which influencers to partner with.

In reality, it is trendy for companies to "offer" free products to manipulate rather than pay customers a flat rate, according to our study. In fact, in exchange for sponsored posts, 77 percent of businesses report giving free products and services.

But this is not always the case. Some influencers accept only flat rates, while others charge for the business based on the number of sales or lead that they create.

9.3 Why Your Business Needs an Instagram Influencer Marketing Strategy?

Instagram is one of the biggest platforms for advertisers to work with influencers and reach new markets fast when it comes to influencer marketing. It is the best performing social action site, with an overall participation level of 3.21 percent (compared with 1.5 percent across all social networks).

A big reason that Instagram influencer marketing is so successful is that it eliminates traditional advertising obstacles and exposes the product to a new audience through your influencer associate, a more trustworthy outlet.

When an influencer recommends on their channels a product or service, it can be seen as an official recommendation from a friend.

Sixty-seven percent of marketers are already using Instagram influencer marketing for promotion—and we expect to see that as organic reach declines, this number will continue to increase.

9.4 Running an Influencer Marketing Campaign

Instagram influencer marketing is rapidly becoming one of the best ways for companies to raise brand awareness, increase their followers, and drive sales— especially as the Instagram algorithm continues to limit organic reach!

Have you not yet tried Instagram's marketing influencer? In this section, we discuss everything from finding the right influencers for your brand, reporting appropriately sponsored posts, and deciding how your influencer marketing tactics work for you:

How much does Instagram Influencer Marketing cost?

There's no doubt that influencers from social media have become famous for product promotions On Instagram in particular! But when there are so many factors to consider, how do you come up with a fair price?

The reality is that influencer marketing rates among influencers still vary widely.

Some influencers reported charging as much as $5000 to $10,000 per sponsored post, according to our 2018 State of Instagram Marketing report. Nonetheless, rates are much more prevalent in the region of $250 to $1000.

Unfortunately, when it comes to how much Instagram influencer marketing costs, there is no one-size-fits-all answer, and there are several factors involved that go far beyond the number of followers of an Instagram influencer.

Thanks to Instagram, the rise of micro-influencer marketing influencer marketing may have grown in popularity, but you may not need thousands of dollars to cash in on this trend.

As a result of a growing trend, more and more companies see the value of partnering with Instagram influencers having a small (or "micro") but highly engaged follow-up. Indeed, according to a Collective report, in 2017, micro-influencers reported growth of 15-75 percent.

So, what's a micro-influencer exactly? Generally speaking, a micro-influencer is someone who follows social media significantly, but not massively. This could range from 1,000 to 100,000 followers from anywhere.

Although influencers of Instagram have gained a form of "celebrity status," micro-influencers are more like ordinary people, and they seem to be very connected and trustworthy. @lauratully.co is a great example. She has been partnering with multiple businesses despite having just over 3000 followers and creating a bunch of sponsored Instagram posts. This is probably due to the niche and engaged following of their industry. As with all Instagram advertising material, by reaching niche audiences, companies will gain a lot.

What's the reason for the increasing number of micro-influencers?

Okay, one of the best benefits of working with micro-influencers is that they appear to maintain higher rates of interaction than influencers of the highest level (According to recent studies, there is a tending negative correlation between participation and audience volume).

While accounts of all sizes are less popular, feedback and followers overall than in the past (thanks to the Instagram algorithm), larger accounts seem to hit a bigger one. But there's also something to tell about how influencers are viewed to different sizes of fans. The truth is that influencers with hundreds of thousands of followers frequently lead lives that aren't necessarily "natural." And if you equate them with someone who has 5000 to 15,000 highly engaged fans on Instagram, who definitely won't pay their rent through cashing in on Instagram sponsorships Okay, it's just much more important to the customer every day!

Indeed, if a micro-influencer features a product on their channels, it may find it more like a friend's trusted recommendation than a celebrity endorsement.

9.5 Effective steps for influencer marketing

Influencer marketing following these steps can be a time-consuming exercise that is difficult to scale to find an influencer and agree on a collaboration with them. Use this five-step process to stay on track for the best results.

1. You're doing your homework.

I can learn so much from other brands. Find out what works for them, get inspiration from the different content types they post, and see what content types get the most engagement. Looking at what competitors are doing is a prominent place to start your research. We use our tool, Whaler Labs, which enables you to see metrics on your Instagram account and compare them with up to three others. Researching other brands, which are not your competitors, but maybe share a similar demographic, is also a good idea. We keep an eye on what Herschel is doing at Shore Projects as we feel that a Herschel customer is also likely to be a customer of Shore Projects. If there's a story behind your brand, research that as well. Our roots come from the British seaside, so we spend a lot of time keeping an eye on accounts based on the shore and the nautical. Finally, Instagram for Business Blog is a good reference point. They post case studies regularly and announce innovations and resources. Reading content specifically about how brands can get the most out of Instagram, is a great place.

2. Set a brief, clear.

The project will be more effective if you encourage the creative freedom influencer to produce content; they know would enjoy their audience. Although mocking a brief with the targets you want to accomplish is equally essential, having creative freedom is one of the main ways to make Instagram's branding influencer effective. Rather than giving the exact image, title, and every last hashtag they have to use, it's better to trust them to build an original and entertaining advertisement for you. A mood board is one file that you could provide with a summary. For Shore Projects, below are descriptions of mood boards that we post. They help to give influencers an idea of the general aesthetics that we like.

3. Choose relevant influencers.

Once you get a clear idea of what you want to do, finding relevant influencers is the next vital step. It can be challenging to get this incorrect, so it's worth investing a little more effort to make the right decision. Nearly every industry has influencers. Whether it's fashion, lifestyle, travel, fitness, more than a few good options are likely to be found. One of the ways to find people is by searching your market for the top Instagram hashtags and looking for highly engaging posts (lots of likes and comments). You can also consider influencers on other companies' pages quite often. Check for articles where someone else is identified as the maker of content. Finding relevant influencers can be quite tricky without spending a long time trawling through hundreds of Instagram accounts, where tools like Whaler come into play. You can search for an influencer database by subject, location, engagement, rates, etc. — all of which are interested in working with relevant brands.

4. Agree on a structure of collaboration.

You will need to reach out to them and agree on a collaborative structure once you have found the influencers you want to work with. There are usually six key aspects you're going to want to work around: Timeframe–stay up-to-date on the timetable and illustrate the need to reach it. Production–be specific about what you want to give them. For instance, two pieces of content, one to be published with a mention of your brand on the influencer's account, and one to be used at your discretion. Usage of content–Let them know what rights you want to use the content. The influencer will always retain ownership as the author, although we usually ask for a license to use the material for a total two-year span. Payment–With their support, almost all of the most influential influencers would demand a fee. Occasionally, as part of that fee, they may be willing to negotiate or take a free product /service/experience; however, you should expect to make some payment. When negotiating a price, remember to pay for multiple services: content creation, rights of use, and access to their audience. Sponsored Hashtag –Sponsored content laws are varying around the globe and are continually changing. I suggest a side caution error and use #spoon or #ad at all times. We find that the output or reaction to the article does not make any difference whatsoever. The goal of the Campaign–Focus clearly on the purpose you are trying to achieve when working with the influencer. That could be as easy as raising your profile followers or pushing visits to your website or brand page through your Instagram bio to increase sales. Knowing what you're working towards as the goal of the campaign keeps both of you aligned.

5. Maximize the quality of the material.

Gain extra value from the Instagram material funded by repurposing it to other platforms. Here are three explanations of ways for Shore Projects to optimize the product value:

Post it on the product page to post the influencer posts on our product pages; we use the Shopify App called Tigray. This not only makes our product pages look great, but it also adds positive social proof and has even led towards the presentation of their content by real customers. We've seen a 23 percent increase in page conversion since we embedded Instagram content, and an impressive 40 percent increase in page time spent.

We discovered that it is essential to keep the ad units updated with new content at a Facebook marketing event. We used our product and lifestyle photography in the beginning and found it very challenging to continue creating new graphics all the time. We are able to refresh our ad units regularly by using influencer content. Also, using influencer content, our conversion rate has improved by 19 percent.

9.6 Connecting with the right influencers

As a direct result of passion and expertise, influencers have authority in specific niches. Hundreds of thousands of followers have been accumulated whose interests align with their niche.

CHAPTER 10: HANDLING FAME (BEING VIRAL)

10.1 Use a monetization tool

When I think about how many e-commerce companies are around these days, I'm more surprised that monetization platforms like Like2Buy or Have2Have. It doesn't take advantage of them. Essentially, these channels allow identifying the items you support on your page simpler for your Instagram followers. Once signed up for one of these programs, make sure that's your bio reference. That way, you can add CTAs to product photos that say things like "Like this look? Shop the link in our bio. "It reduces a visitor's effort to become a customer, and that's always a good thing.

10.2 Partner up with supporters

Influencers are people with influence with a significant following.

Partnership with such individuals to support your company would allow you to create an extensive network and bring your product to markets that might otherwise have been unavailable. Conversions are significantly affected by a "shout-out" for your brand from an influencer. Why?

The result is that consumers rarely turn to brands as sources of factual information or reviews. When push comes to shove, buyers trust influences more than a "tooting their own horn" brand. Use analytics tools such as Ninja outreach or TrendSpottr to find influencers in your niche faster.

Close a list of goals and send a free (or trial) version of your product. Be sure to ask influencers if they like your product to mention your brand organically in a post. She dropped a reference to a Lo & Sons handbag when fashion stylist SaniaDemina was preparing for a trip to New York. The article was presented in a way that did not seem to be pay-promotion, but rather an initial and genuine analysis of a valued brand.

Partnering with NGOs is another way to promote the product with the aid of others.
Millennial buyers are socially conscious and like to work with companies that are socially responsible or have a good impact on the environment.

If your brand is donating to a campaign or causing it to align with the values and mission of your customer, you will attract their attention and form strong emotional links.

It's your aim here to gain community sympathy and manipulate opinions.

Don't try to measure commitment or ROI, or you're going to look disingenuous.

Even if your brand is not officially associated with a charity, there are other ways you can contribute, such as sending employees on community service trips or holding fundraisers. Only note to refresh the photos of your fans. Toyota USA partnered with America's Boys and Girls Club, where the latter would receive $50 each time a follower posts a selfie using the hashtag #selflessie.

10.3 Running contests

Lastly-the best-kept secret. While competitions on Instagram are standard, running a thematic hashtag contest helps you create a single, coherent campaign. Create a campaign-specific hashtag (e.g. "#WishpondSummer2017") and get entries to post photos by the hashtag and tag your brand in your picture itself. Contests are fun for your company and can help you grow social support quickly.

If so inclined, you can run your contest on an external page to generate information for your enterprise to which you can market by email in the future. When that isn't quite your cup of tea, you still can look to host a third-party hashtag contest, so you have an impressive gallery of entries. Moreover, you can follow your competition, which means you can reach these interested fans in the future.

An Instagram competition is a fun way to win followers and increase engagement.

Nikon even developed a complete Instagram account for its Nikon Photo Contest 2016-2017. However, make sure you have time to set up and monitor the contest to ensure it is successful, and the participants are glad. The overall purpose should be to increase your commitment and drag post (and your brand) to your attention.

- The game must have rules

- Participation must be pure (ask users to like the post or follow your page)

- hold competitions regularly to increase chances that it becomes viral often

- Including a reward

- Use a similar hashtag. It's a good idea to use a licensed person.

Do not forget to build an exciting chart to share the contest with people who entered after it ends and thank them for participating.

How to run an Instagram contest?

The Instagram contest is, and for a good reason, a particularly popular social network technique. They can deliver great results because they all love the opportunity to win something.

Instagram **contest rules** to remember. It's good to do a quick refresher course on the contest rules of Instagram before you start your Instagram contest. You can find them here.

You can't in any way suggest that Instagram is associated with the competition.

Users can not be asked to mark themselves or others in pictures in which they are not.

You follow local laws and standards, including gender, qualifications, or award limitations.

- **The rules for entry and participation must be clearly stated**.

Types of contests that can run On Instagram, you can run numerous different kinds of games. Each offers its unique advantages, and for maximized results and ROI, many merchants will overlap different contest concepts.

• **Tag friends in the comments:** This is supposed to have new followers draw their friends who might theoretically be interested in your business. It's not for any product, but it's user-friendly and takes little effort. It will give you an enormous bump in commitment, as well.

• **Follow us**: This is a part of contest participation rather than the sole requirement of users, but it is often the underlying goal of many merchants. After all, a one-time statement isn't wrong, but it's better to follow the long term.

• **Leave a comment**: these contests take the form of subtitle contests, or users may be asked to leave their opinion and share the experience. These contests are to track, and you are likely to get plenty of participation because the entry barrier is low.

• **Photo contests**: maybe the most challenging time for users, these contests also yield the highest rewards (and therefore require the most attractive prizes). Users are expected to upload an original image or video, whether natively attached to a hashtag competition or via contest software. They provide the most valuable UGC you can use later on your profile.

Software contest: Should merchants use it?

Before starting your contest, decide whether to use contest software. There are both pros and cons of using it.

Using competition technology can cost money (typically about $30-50 a month), so putting together more time would take because you need to build landing pages. This often ensures that your Instagram competition won't "work" native; visitors won't be able to comment on a single post, they'll need to tap and participate in the reference in your profile.

That said, using contest software has significant advantages. Tracking participants and their entries make it much easier to choose a winner. Some contest software can even select a random winner for you. Often, you can get outstanding metrics to see how the competition is measuring up with targets, often in real-time. Want to add a voting element to the contest? You can do it now. Due to the safe competition landing page, you can even get real lead information, including client phone numbers or email addresses. It offers you factual, quantifiable lead data that can be used later to cultivate leads or retarget them.

If you choose the contest software, I recommend the following services:

- Short Stack

- Wish pond

- Woo box

10.4 Finding a unique and creative voice

Hold the statistics in mind when taking pictures or videos for sharing on Instagram.

Anyone visiting your page will get an instant impression of the identity of your brand, so you need to present yourself exactly how you want to be perceived. And pictures of low quality won't cut it. You want to look professional, so be sure to display high-resolution images from Noisy Water Winery like these. Moreover, since Instagram users are likely to view your account from a mobile phone, any flawed or dark pictures on their screens will look even worse.

Nonetheless, you don't have to be a master in Photoshop to have beautiful pictures. With a tool like Canva, you can easily create some high-quality images. Your page's content should be unique to your speech. Be unique in your industry and showcase your perspective, and your audience will appreciate your authenticity.

Try to match the posts in your feed somewhat, so each of your pictures has a similar feel. Here's how we're doing it on our homepage. So long, so you add something to the dialogue and offer credit when credit is due, the photographs must not be original. Post quotes or even news stories regarding popular topics in the industry and make your message to start a conversation with those seeing the share.

Psychologically verified videos with a lot of red colors deter a fan from moving. Nonetheless, blue pictures receive 24% more views than red ones. When creating a theme, keep that in mind: bluer, less red. This will attract the attention of people and increase their chances of becoming viral. Tags are another great way to get in touch with people on Instagram and get exposure.

10.5 Increasing the fame

Viral content can bring your brand to the next level, especially if your post goes on social media viral Imagine the impact of tens of thousands and millions on your social job opportunities. Quite fantastic! You may believe it's challenging to get viral, but I'm here to say it to you— it isn't. A simple guide can be used for viral purposes by anyone. The following tips and tricks will help you move in the right direction in your social media. If you want a viral post, you need to know what initially triggers sharing. It is analyzed 100 million jobs in 2014 to look for patterns in most shared content. Some or all of these features had the most shared content: Invoked awe, laughter, or fun Appealed to the narcissistic side of people – made them look smart to share the New York Times surveyed 2500 people to find out why they posted an online story. Our articles or blog posts from trusted sources. The main reasons for this were: bringing valuable and entertaining content to one another, identifying oneself for others (giving people a better awareness of who they are) improving and empathic relationships (staying connected with others) to self-fulfillment (to be more involved in the world) A study found people shared with: Give-offers, or discounts Advise-tips, helpful hints Warn-potential dangers Amuse –entertaining content Inspire-images and quotes Amaze-pictures and facts Unite-be part of the tribe So while there were some differences, there's a fair amount of overlap in these lists. So, the first viral lesson in 2016 was to ensure that some of these reasons are taped into your content.

There are outliers of viral posts. They're not the norm; they're outstanding. To identify what the typical share count is, we have analyzed over 500 million articles. Most content is getting very few shares. To control your goals in 2016, the average is eight shares! This even extends to the very most prominent viral pages. Their top posts would outperform the majority of their material significantly. Their viral posts are outliers, even for Buzz Feed and its competitors.

CHAPTER 11: REACTIONS AND REVIEWS

11.1 Run your Instagram audit

With your ambitions and target in mind, the next move is by doing an Instagram review to take a critical look at your Instagram profile.

By doing so, you're going to take a critical look at everything you've done so far on the platform, analyze it, and then decide whether it still serves your business ' needs. (Even if you're starting marketing with Instagram, running an audit is an excellent opportunity to make sure you're on the right track.) Each element of your Instagram profile should be deliberate, including your photo profile, bio, feed, captions, hashtags, and more.

Also, your current accounts on Instagram are part of your product. Will you find inspiration for them? Align with your company? Or are they completely disconnected and random?

Remember to keep goals in mind and to audit your account to make sure you're closer to them with any decision you make!

After the conclusion of your Instagram assessment, you should have:

- Defined goals and objectives of your Instagram companies

- A clear understanding of your identity and speech

- Strengthened design of your posts

- Assessed your latest communication plan

- Refined your hashtag strategy

11.2 Testimonials and reviews of followers

Social proof can mean anything when it comes to making purchase decisions. If you're trying to use Instagram as a way to drive your business sales, consumer testimonials and feedback is another great idea for content. Saying that your product is the best is one thing-but showing potential customers what other people are saying can help build your brand's positive perception of the customer.

Upload a related image with text added on top or in the caption and add in the picture and upload the person you are referencing. If you are a local business, it can be even more useful to post video testimonials. Adding to your arsenal is the first type of content.

As a consequence, businesses need to be more conscious of when their use is most interested in Instagram so that they can schedule their content to surface at that moment.

How do you know the accounts on your feed? When you regularly post on the pictures of someone or get associated with them in images, it indicates to Instagram that they fall into the category of "friends and family." As a consequence, you'll see more content posted by them (and vice versa!).

For businesses, this is excellent news because it gives them a way to remain top-of-mind. Just ask your followers to tag you in their posts and make sure you optimize your posts and stories on Instagram to get as many comments as you can.

CHAPTER 12: TIPS AND TRICKS

12.1 Assign someone to monitor messaging channels

On a variety of social media platforms, many consumers expect to receive almost instant customer support. Also, the average person will share with 16 of their friends the story of a negative customer service experience.

As Instagram grows in popularity, providing adequate customer support will be increasingly crucial for brands of all sizes. And since Instagram Business accounts give viewers on profiles with the ability to contact brands with the touch of a button, requests for customer service could quickly come at any time of day.

Given this reality, marketers in social media should consider assigning someone during working hours to monitor incoming Instagram messages.

12.2 Keep post draft on hand

If you're still unsure about investing time and money in a scheduling app, don't be afraid-you'll find a solution. Selections are an unknown feature in Instagram. Write a comment and include people in it when you submit an image to the web, but choose not to post it yet. You can instead choose to save your post as a draft. It stores the position (edits and all) in the browser, helping you to pull it up automatically the next time you want to publish it.

Although it's not as lovely as scheduling a tee for your material, it's still a great way to keep some ready-to-go content on deck. If it's a little more spontaneous to find your Instagram strategy, drafts are a great feature to have.

12.3 Don't be afraid to stir things up

Not all posts on social media need to be fluffy to engage and share with people. If jobs do not resonate with the audience, it may be time to move from fluffy to controversial. If you need to stir things up, post that you have a favorable view about something divisive happening in the world. The goal is to emotionalize because people love sharing emotional content and letting their voices be heard.

For example, if I don't feel a particularly controversial topic in the news, or even a trend in human behavior, I'll post something about it.

12.4 Socialize well with existing followers

The word "social" in social media marketing is often forgotten by users and brands. All they're focusing on is posting, enhancing visibility, and increasing reach.

You must not fail to engage adequately with your fans and potential customers as a maker.

Responding to tweets, promoting shares, and telling them to add related friends are some ways to communicate and build trust with them.

Socializing on the business account is an excellent growth strategy for Instagram as it supports the creation of loyal organic followers. Therefore, people want to be heard and respected to respond well, and to engage them in discussion encourages them to share their content and profile.

12.5 Use Instagram Live to Tease New Products

To use Instagram Live, many businesses are understandably hesitant. For many people, the idea of "living" on Instagram is pretty daunting. While Instagram Stories offers you the option of pre-recorded video publishing, Instagram Live does not have "retakes." The truth is, though, that Instagram Live has tremendous business value. The feature can be an incredible channel to drive new followers and engagement as well as your broader business goals when used correctly. This is why we see a recent trend in businesses using the platform to threaten or launch new goods

12.6 Leaving nothing blank

This seems obvious, but you must be sure that your profile is complete. You want to be as credible as you can. That also means filling out the dreaded section "About Me." Your Instagram account should also be linked to your Facebook account. Decide if you want to link your Instagram to a Facebook personal or business, or create a page for the sole purpose of showcasing Instagram activity. It's up to you, but if you already have connections on your Facebook business page, linking your Instagram for maximum exposure is probably wise. It's a good idea to say that all the pictures follow a similar pattern.

13. CONCLUSIONS

You've made it to the end if you're reading this far. Hopefully, you've absorbed enough from the Instagram advertising tips, which I've discussed with you on Instagram marketing may be overwhelming and challenging, yet you can quickly transform tourists into fans and consumers with the right emphasis and long-term dedication.

Here's what you need to remember:

- Create particular customized pages that add value to your followers

- Test different content formats to appease different types of followers

- Allow yourself a breathtaking room with multiple targeted accounts

- Make your audience feel special to keep coming back for more

- Find willing supporters that paint your brand with positive organic light.

But you need to know how to use it to love other accounts. We haven't won our next Instagram in one day, but Rome wasn't built in one day either.

With the aid of our technology and a few shortcuts, you'll have a viral Instagram post on your hands in no time. Be sure to complete your Instagram profile, so people know you're legit to be featured on the "Top Posts" page.

Upload pictures that fit the theme of your brand and use tags and emoji to increase your exposure chances.

Promote a viral image as an ad and upload it only when your users are active. With your planning tool, plan your articles.

Find and share your content with influencers.

And don't forget to run competitions to share your picture with your friends on your blogs. Instagram continues to develop, grow, and evolve as a marketing platform, creating effective marketing strategies for Instagram is more important than ever for businesses. And that requires a thorough understanding of the advertising environment of Instagram so actual observations into what is useful and what is not.

Businesses of all kinds have so much to gain from building a presence on Instagram at the end of the day, whether it's growing a committed community, reaching new customers, or even selling e-commerce. This needs just a little energy!

If you're thinking about taking your Instagram marketing seriously, enlisting the help of Later, a free marketing platform for Instagram is a good idea.

Not only you can plan feed and manage all photos and videos with Later, but also be able to track analytics and automatically schedule Instagram posts — all from a single dashboard!

14. REFERENCES

1. **Marketing basics**

    https://blog.wishpond.com/post/115675437381/instagram-marketing-secrets

    https://later.com/instagram-marketing/

2. **Targeting and engagements**

    https://www.vreeland.com/delve/find-engage-grow-audience-instagram-ad-free/

    https://sproutsocial.com/insights/instagram-target-audience/

3. **Growing business(marketing)**

    https://www.shopify.com/blog/instagram-marketing

    https://www.jeffbullas.com/29-tips-on-how-to-succeed-with-your-instagram-marketing-infographic/

4. **Advertisement**

    https://www.shopify.com/blog/instagram-ads

5. **Viral**

    https://digitalmarketinginstitute.com/blog/7-ways-make-content-go-viral

6. **Marketing team**

https://www.jeffbullas.com/digital-marketing-team/
https://www.outbrain.com/blog/successful-digital-marketing-team/

7. **Profile optimization**

https://www.entrepreneur.com/article/309671

www.ingramcontent.com/pod-product-compliance
Lightning Source LLC
Chambersburg PA
CBHW070633220526
45466CB00001B/165